WOMEN ON FILM

WOMEN ON FILM

The Critical Eye

Marsha McCreadie

PRAEGER SPECIAL STUDIES • PRAEGER SCIENTIFIC

Library of Congress Cataloging in Publication Data

McCreadie, Marsha, date
   Women on film.

   Bibliography: p.
   Includes index.
   1. Women motion picture critics.
2. Moving-picture criticism. I. Title.
PN1995.M377   1982   791.43 01 50922 82-13221
ISBN 0–03–062768–0
    0–03–071737–X pb

Published in 1983 (hb) and 1984 (pb) by Praeger Publishers
CBS Educational and Professional Publishing
a Division of CBS Inc.
521 Fifth Avenue, New York, NY 10175, U.S.A.

456789 052 987654321

Printed in the United States of America

No one ever built a monument to a critic

—*Anon.*

Acknowledgments

A work like this incurs many debts. The most obvious one is to the women film critics who allowed themselves to be interviewed: Molly Haskell, Janet Maslin, Marjorie Rosen, and Nora Sayre. Others, like Lotte Eisner, Jan Dawson, and Laura Mulvey were generously responsive in correspondence. A number of scholars helped in a variety of ways. Professors Virginia Tiger and Bruce Franklin of Rutgers University in Newark, New Jersey, were encouraging in early stages of the manuscript's preparation. Professor Robert Carringer of the University of Illinois and Professor Alan Spiegel of SUNY at Buffalo read the manuscript in rough draft and helped to draw out some of the finer points. Professor Don Staples of North Texas State provided specialized information. Independent scholar Charlotte Mandel was uncommonly generous in sharing her work on H.D. Professor Jim Welsh of *Literature/Film Quarterly* has continued to provide support.

The Secretarial Center of Iona College in New Rochelle was unvaryingly patient and prompt; special thanks to Nancy Girardi. Lynda Sharp has been an interested and cheerful editor. Thanks too to Eric Jensen and William O'Rourke: oldest and best of critics.

Marsha McCreadie
New York City, May 1982

Contents

Introduction

It's strikingly easy to come up with vast numbers of women who have written about the cinema. The other gender, too, though for some reason their names don't spring so readily to mind. For unlike areas in which women are only now gaining ground, or really taking hold, women film critics, reviewers, and historians have been at it for a very long time. For once we don't need to self-consciously catalogue the "break-throughs" that women have made in the arena of film explication, or to madly search for prominent women in the field. Quite simply, women were first on the reviewing scene. And it is a continuing tradition, for women critics and historians have been prominent throughout all phases and areas of film art, unlike any other. (A fact that led one male critic to sourly wonder if "the matriarchy . . . may not have had the un-fortunate side-effect of planting, deep in the collective unconscious, the notion that in order to review films it is necessary to be womanly," *The Observer*, November 29, 1964). Not of course, to be freely retrospective, that anyone thought the scene was going to be quite so important.

A nicer trick, however—especially with the present self-consciousness about women's issues—is to explain the magnetic field marked out by the cinema, criticism, and women writers. Criticism by its very nature is once removed, they say. And women in our culture have been trained to be apart: passive observers or vicarious partakers. Yet women critics achieved superstar status in the 1960s and early-1970s at a time when both the women's movement and film were in full tide.

Still, there are some easy socio-historical answers to give in figur-ing the numbers, if not the importance, of women who have written about film. Film reviewing was originally considered a second-rate activ-ity: in embarrassment, early journalist-critics wrote about movies under pseudonyms, so it's not unlikely that the cinema could have been a throwaway for women. In fact, early reviews often appeared on the "women's page" of a daily newspaper, being thought not important enough to take up time and space in the more commercially clout-rich drama section.

Another easy guess is the fact that the cinema and mass art share roots. If women are an oppressed group or at least not part of the ruling class in Western culture, the attraction to a "lively," democratic, and as-yet-not-rigidly codified art form would be natural. Here, too, the ready availability and relative cheapness of film (in most of the world if no longer in England) made it a less formidable art form than others. The wittily irreverent Iris Barry, early British film critic and first film cura-tor of New York's Museum of Modern Art, observes in one of her books that movies are cheap, available, and a popular rather than a social art, and then relievedly concludes "you don't have to put your best clothes on to see Harold Lloyd fall off a sky-scraper" (*Let's Go to the Movies,* 1925). And with no long bibliography of male names attached to a study of the cinema, women possibly felt less intimidated about dipping their toes into these critical waters.[1]

More sophisticated arguments might hold that woman is attracted to an art form that may be seen as nonmainstream even in its aesthetic format: although narrative and plot make a strong appeal, it is within the framework of a "new" view of time and space. Nonlinear thought provides freedom from (patriarchal) hierarchy and rigidity. The insight that the cinema's free and simultaneous use of space and time is analogous to the "modern" temper is not new, but film, with its nonverticality, may have provided women with an alternative to what Virginia Woolf saw as "male" forms (her example was the linear masculine sentence of the nineteenth-century essay).[2] If the writer's "I" automatically implies isolation as much as the phallocentric pen, one other thing is certain: you can go to the movies alone. Here life and art conveniently married for women in American culture anyway, which stressed—up until the late 1960s and early-1970s—the pariah-like character of the woman by herself. Film provided the perfect equivalent for isolation: and no one need know. Especially if cinema-going could be kept to "off-hours." For even with a companion, the moviegoer is always alone, once the lights go off.

The privacy, the passivity, particularly the dream-like state of film-going has been noted by so many critics and reviewers that it might hint at one of the "real" shared attractions of women to the cinema. The easy slide into appreciating—or apprehending at very least—an art that takes one over, as both Alfred Hitchcock and Robert Altman have suggested, is perfect for women who have been trained to wait for something (really, some*one*) to overwhelm them.

A related issue is the illusion of power that takes the film critic out of the world of "mere" vicarious identification and into the realm of omnipotence. And for woman deprived of power, control, and often even of ease in her daily life, film is more than just vicarious satisfaction: it is substitute gratification. Release from sublimation draws woman to the screen like a magnet. Dream analogies in the sense of wish-fulfillments quite naturally apply (and surface frequently in the work of women critics). The analogy was so obvious for critic Renata Adler that when she was reviewing for the *New York Times,* her favorite screening time was 8:00 AM, when the "change to the movie world was entirely smooth" (*A Year in the Dark*). Yet it's clearly more than just the similarity of the darkened theater to sleep, for other analogies might work as readily. The movie house is womb-like, cave-like, and so on. But dreams—with parallel images and seeming illogic—are the recurring leitmotif. The dreamer is, of course, always at the center of the dream. And, as we see particularly in the work of a critic like Pauline Kael, this center of consciousness rarely lets go of center-stage.

The cinema critic is moreover the director's director, the actor's mentor, the photographer's eye. All without the distressing responsibility of having the individuals in question present: the burden of the drama critic. And, one might conjecture, the possibility of "real" events backfiring on an untutored controller. While it often seems that film critics show a proclivity to rewrite or control their subject matter, women critics—when compared with men reviewers like James Agee, Stanley Kauffmann, or Dwight Macdonald—tend to adjust cinematic reality in their reviews and articles to a much greater extent. Displacement of the lack of control in other areas is the easy psychological explanation, and has led current *New York Times* reviewer Janet Maslin to call film critics an "odd bunch" in that it can be "very satisfying to be both immediately involved and yet removed" (in a May 1979 interview).

Interestingly, women's attraction to film has resulted in some totally original theoretical approaches. Perhaps the biggest surprise is to come across a kind of precocious auteur theory. Early British critics [Winifred Ellerman] Bryher and C.A. [Caroline] Lejeune concentrate on directors in their books *Film Problems of Soviet Russia* (1929) and *Cinema* (1931). So does Iris Barry in her brightly chatty *Let's Go to the Movies*. But it is Lejeune who declares, in a review for the London *Observer,* that she is all for "dictatorship in film-making" by relying on a director "whose signature on the film represents final and incomparable authority" (January 12, 1941).

Yet their "discovery" of some kernel of the auteur theory is perhaps not so unexpected after all. Schooled to see art as produced by men, it's really no wonder that women managed very early to perceive that it might be one (male) individual who was responsible for the final cinematic creation. Although for more self-conscious feminists, like critic Marjorie Rosen, the auteur theory is automatically chauvinistic not only because it concentrates solely on male directors, but also in that it "does not take into account spur-of-the-moment, collaborative [read feminist collective] decisions" (in an August 1978 interview).

Women critics have broken ground in other theoretical areas, as well. Lejeune, Pauline Kael, feminists Molly Haskell and Marjorie Rosen, and occasional writers on the cinema Simone de Beauvoir and Colette among others, have all posited the possibility that an actor, actress, or "star" could—consciously or not—have control over the selection of their roles. (By logical extension, of course, on the audience too.) This approach might be seen as some combination of psychobiography and auteurism for actors. In fact Colette, in writing about Mae West in 1934, even uses the word "auteur." For Beauvoir it is when "the actor turns himself once and for all into the amalgam of one particular character: on the screen, the distance between Mr. Chaplin and Charlie is entirely done away with" (*All Said and Done*). Chaplin and Brando are naturals for this method, and Kael and Lejeune both have essays regarding these extraordinary figures in this fashion. Others gave intellectual credence and theoretical underpinnings to seeing an actor's combined roles as ouevre and to analyzing how the cinematic myth of a star can affect the national psyche. French critic Claude-Edmonde Magny and American anthropologist Hortense Powdermaker make use of and dignify this approach, which was formerly thought of as frivolous.

And though it seems that it was mainly in the last decade that we worried about cinematic role models for women, or a feminist theory for the cinema, both Barry and Lejeune complained—in 1925 and 1926 respectively—of film's "apparently meaningless, immensely conventional love interests," which insist in ending with marriage—the beginning, according to Barry, of difficulties rather than the end; that instead of showing the woman viewer horses, the director, Lejeune says, "gives her children; for adventure, domesticity; for the gun, a Paris gown." Colette in 1935 praises Mae West for giving us heroines both impudent and not unhappily solitary.

Women writers on the cinema are no slouches in other theoretical departments either. All the world knows the work of aesthetician, novelist, and screenwriter Susan Sontag, but she is not the only woman theorist to discuss the "inter-penetration" of film and the arts, or to analyze the formal, "self-contained" qualities of film; both of these concerns may be found in the work of Annette Michelson, the flamboyant film critic and teacher, dubbed (by critic Vlada Petric) a twentieth-century Tartuffe. Many critics have compared film with other arts, but the very large proportion of women using this approach seems to suggest a greater degree of openness to possible interconnections and cross-fertilizations. Magny and Sontag are particularly fine on the interrelationships with literature, Michelson and German-born critic Lotte Eisner make extensive use of their training in art history to analyze the visual elements in film.

Women critics seem to have an affinity with and admiration for the cinema's "romantic" ability to fix or alter time. This was well understood by Virginia Woolf early on and can be found in the work of Sontag and in the theoretical writings of Maya Deren, the pioneer woman film maker, as well. Deren's work may be said to have set some aesthetic boundaries for the poetic or avant-garde film; providing what might be seen as an opposite approach is the work of Eisner or Penelope Houston, who can comprehensively capture the "sweep" of a national cinema.

In fact, many women film critics apply a vaguely sociological approach, perhaps because it seemed as if no formal apparatus was required, and the cinema provided raw material for "instant sociology." For *Times* reviewer Maslin, "theory can get in the way of a direct response to things" and she likes "as little between me and the subject matter as possible." No one is more at ease with the ready generalization than Pauline Kael, though poet H.D., writing in an early *Close Up*, and critic Bryher, nearly match her. And while film, of all the arts, seems to elicit a personal response, nearly autobiographical reactions to the cinema can be observed in the work of many of these critics. Some see themselves standing for the culture at large—as writers have tended to do since nineteenth-century romanticism. Occasional writer on film Joan Didion is a clear example of a writer who sees herself as a culturally paradigmatic receptor of the message of movies. American feminists Molly Haskell, Marjorie Rosen, and Joan Mellen necessarily take both a loosely sociological and personal approach; if their work is weak in rigorous theory compared to a British feminist like Laura Mulvey, one can say in their defense that they were the first American women film critics to have single-handedly written full-length books of criticism.

A few women film critics make use of a "sociological" approach to attack a political system they see as oppressive. Leftist or Marxist thought can be observed in the work of critics as different as Mulvey, Mellen, and Bryher, as well as of Sontag and Michelson. But the cinema doesn't attract just radical politics (although a case may be made for this): long-time film reviewer Judith Crist is no progressive, and Dilys Powell, critic of the *London Times* for nearly 40 years, is apolitical if anything.

All the women film critics treated here are wonderfully descriptive and able to fix on the "telling" detail, from writers as different as Crist or Kael, to reviewers Nora Sayre, Janet Maslin, and Renata Adler. The specificity, the multiplicity of detail of the cinema invites an extraordinary focus on the particular, as we can see in the work of James Agee, criticized not infrequently for concentrating too much on the parts rather than the whole. (His enthusiasts defend him by saying that he was so in love with movies that he lost distance, and perspective.) Missing the forest for the trees is a more common complaint about women critics and reviewers, a censure that ironically depends on women's superior abilities to perceive details (one of the few sex differences that psychologists and physiologists have agreed on).[3]

Of course women who write about film have their particular flaws; and in their different as well as shared faults they cover just about every writer's tic: prose that is loquacious, rambling, often undisciplined, and obsessive and erratic at times. But these are traits of the brand new, of the partisan, rather than of women. For the objectivity of Powdermaker, the finely reasoned argumentation of Sontag, the careful scholarship of

Eileen Bowser, disprove any sexist arguments about a woman's inability to coolly analyze and organize.

Perhaps, too, some of the conditioning that accrues to "growing up female" has, for once, been turned into a vocational aid. Women critics, because of an at least partial lifetime of having to pick up on the moods of others (was this why we were always called intuitive?) can be extraordinary when discussing an actor or director. *New Yorker* critic Penelope Gilliatt explains her critical method: "one has to love and admire and have pondered over the subject's work and cast of mind" (introduction to *Three-Quarter Face*). And they were earlier, too, than their male counterparts in expressing a real sense of audience, or—in today's academic jargon—audience response. Here it is tempting to cite the most recent psychological findings that show that females, even as infants, respond more strongly than men do to people's faces; they have a higher degree of "interpersonal sensitivity."[4]

Moreover, traditional feminine "disability" with technical matters is somewhat disproven by observing women writers catching on very early to cinematic visual techniques: Virginia Woolf's 1926 essay "The Movies and Reality" foretells a number of cinematic techniques like surrealistic images and imaginative cross-cutting. Montage, too, although she doesn't use this word. Poet Marianne Moore, in a review for *Close Up*, the first film journal, founded in 1927, refers to a kind of cinematic superimposition. H.D. (Hilda Doolittle), the imagist poet, fully understands some very technical aspects of editing, as her pamphlet on the film *Borderline* as well as her film reviews for *Close Up* show. Nor—except for the references to sleep and dreaming—does one discover in women's writing on the cinema recurrent motifs like the imagery of confinement that has been discerned in other work by women. Perhaps the far-ranging narrative, spatial, and visual possibilities of film have counteracted the tendency for women to respond in terms of their own (previous) personal limitations.

In any cataloguing and compiling there are bound to be arbitrary categories that overlap, or seem to make others not as important. People don't "fit" or they fit in too many places. If a fault is to be assigned here, it's the organizer's, although a multiplicity of critical interests among women film critics is one excuse. More painful are the omissions. Without being apologetic—many fine critics and writers aren't discussed here. Current critics Cecile Starr, Arlene Croce, Marsha Kinder, and Annette Insdorf are all writers among many others who deserve equal time.

Still, at the very least, I hope that this book will shed some light on women writers who have gotten lost in the shuffle, and will remind us of the work of others who are more well-known. The most extraordinary women, to me, were/are those who wrote major articles or books while also putting into practice in reviews what they were advocating in their longer work. But let the reader decide, as these women have, on the state of the movies, and criticism.

NOTES

1. For a discussion of the paralyzing effect of predecessors on writers, particularly for women, see Chapter 2 of *The Madwoman in the Attic: The Woman Writer and the Nineteenth Century Imagination,* Sandra Gilbert and Susan Gubar, eds. (New Haven and London: Yale University Press, 1979).

2. *A Room of One's Own.*

3. Robert May, *Sex and Fantasy: Patterns of Male and Female Development* (New York: W.W. Norton, 1980). Also see *Exploring Sex Differences,* Lloyd and Archer, eds. (New York: Academic Press, 1976).

4. Maggie Scarf, *Unfinished Business: Pressure Points in the Lives of Women* (New York: Doubleday, 1980). Also see "Infants' Response to Facial Stimuli During the First Years of Life," *Developmental Pyschology I* (1969): 75-86; and Carol Gilligan, *In a Different Voice* (Cambridge, Mass.: Harvard University Press, 1982).

1

New Yorker Niceties:

Pauline Kael and Penelope Gilliatt

With the possible exception of John Simon, whose readership is much narrower, no contemporary American critic has managed to stir readers as consistently as Pauline Kael has. In Kael's case, however, her strong, controversial opinions, her argumentativeness, are mitigated by her charm, wit, and enthusiasm. A clever use of slang, integrated with a wide—her detractors would say not deep—knowledge of movies has been her hallmark. Her work is shot through with an irascibility, and a not-so-careful anger (there is really no other word for it) that is still somehow fun to read, as Simon's irritations so often are not. Agreement with Kael's view on the part of the reader is rarely the point, although familiarity with it is obligatory enough. Since the early 1970s, "Pauline says" has been a conversational opener among members of some circles that assumed the listener's awareness if not interest. And although her references may be nostagically based in the 1930s, or her sentimentality too hokily expressed for the most sophisticated taste, her emotional commitment to movies (as she insists upon the distinction from "film"), her moralizing certainty about them, went unquestioned. Yet high-priestess oracle she's not; nor would she want to be thus regarded. The ease with which we refer to her—albeit archly—by her first name attests to the ready familiarity she has purposefully set up: at best a free-wheeling mannerist populism pervades her image—and at worst a kind of strong-arming, along the lines of an intellectual George Wallace.

In considering Kael, however, there have always been rumblings about repetitiveness, favoritism, and a lack of a consistent theory. Other complaints came from "true cinephiles" who pointed out Kael's lack of visual sensibility and an overly heavy reliance on literary references. And in the summer of 1980, in the frame of reviews of her most recent book, *When the Lights Go Down*, these complaints coalesced as critics

Andrew Sarris in the *Village Voice* and Renata Adler in the *New York Review of Books* took Kael to task with diatribes consisting of cleverly nasty personal reminiscences, and accusations that Kael's aesthetics rest on sexual sadism, respectively. Both pieces had an unattractive dog-in-the-manger quality: Sarris saw Kael as a hectoring and—he's careful to point out—older hag, while Adler portrayed her as off her sexual rocker. But the real disgruntled zinger seemed to be that Kael had obtained a year-long leave of absence from *The New Yorker* to work in Hollywood in film production (advising Warren Beatty), a double irony since it was about studio "heads" and the industry in general that Kael had always been the most critical. With typical insouciance, she shrugged off surprise at her temporary decampment, explaining that after 30 years of doing one thing—criticism—she needed a change as much as anyone else. She subsequently managed to return to her column at will, with a great deal of anticipation from readers and fellow critics alike. And with what must be to other writers an irritating facileness, almost a fickleness, she turned her Hollywood excursion—which certainly might be regarded as a flop—into a column using her "new" information about the industry to condemn it vitriolically.

But it's doubtful that Kael, or any writer, no matter how successful at self-promotion, would provoke such extreme reactions over the long haul without the extraordinary base she, and for a good long decade, Penelope Gilliatt shared at *The New Yorker.* Few American magazines have as much cultural clout and cachêt as this one does. Its editorial policy is every writer's dream, with floating deadlines, high pay, and practically nonexistent editorial interference. Furthermore, publication in *The New Yorker* implies both mainstream and highbrow acceptance, for the bulk and variety of its advertising (which has been a long-standing joke for being so much at odds with the editorial content) tells even the most casual observer that the magazine has more than a parochial, northeastern appeal. It is extremely prestigious to hook on to its editorial staff early in life, as critic-at-large Brendan Gill did, moving from one arts-reviewing spot to another. But it is surely more impressive to be "brought in" from the outside, to be so well established that the editorial finger beckons from within. And there is no doubt that for many *New Yorker* readers the stylistic and thematic counterpoint of Kael and Gilliatt was one of the primary reasons for buying the magazine. For, except for certain nearly unquestioning loyalties that they hold for individual directors and actors, it would be a challenge to find two more different writers (was this what *New Yorker* editor William Shawn had in mind?). And while extollers of one critic might find fault with the other, at least there was always something to please each camp.

Even so, there is no question that the latitude given its writers by the magazine brought out the worst as well as the best in each critic.

Kael's gargantuan loves and hates expanded with each obsession, trailing her column along with her, and Gilliatt's reviews often took a wildly free form—sometimes with wonderful autonomy, though often with a hauteur that seemed not unwilling to ignore her reader's ease. Enthusiasts found her criticism brilliantly, imaginatively descriptive—to use her word, "evocative"—while others saw it often so far afield from the film(s) under scrutiny as to render those works unrecognizable. This was most evident when Gilliatt used scenariolike or free associational first-person narration in her reviews.

Yet Kael's sometimes pedestrian recounting of a film's narrative plus nearly "in-house" gossip, which was irritating to some readers, was neutralized by Gilliatt's rarefied sensibility and seemingly snobbish appeal. What Gilliatt likes about movies, generally, is their alignment with classical values, although in a perverse and eclectic way, she often seems to choose lesser-known films to comment on. She can be convincingly rhapsodic, sometimes wildly reverential, when explaining the merits of a "great" director: a Jacques Tati, a Truffaut, a formerly unappreciated master like Abel Gance, or a contemporary auteur like Woody Allen. Not infrequently, she will go to bat for a film she sees as representative of the American popular culture (as a Briton, mainstream U.S. culture is especially interesting to her). And whether describing "high" or "low" films, her elliptical, frequently metaphorical comparisons seem just— inexplicably—right. However, her references, whether culturally comparative or based on personal acquaintance with various directors and actors, do tend to name-drop. And they are far too highbrow.

This snobbery is rarely associated with Kael, who admires films and actors who have a broader appeal, and will go to rhetorical lengths to defend the work of someone she considers vital, "pop," even "pulpy." This approach is canonized in Kael's essay "Trash, Art, and the Movies," first published in *Harper's* in February 1969, a piece that many believe turned film criticism back to its populist roots. It insists that movies not be looked at as elitist art, to be rigidly codified or academically classified. Moreover, to really find the "art" of cinema (which she never defines) we must first declare our enjoyment of "trash." Whatever else she has or hasn't done to or for film criticism, Kael must be credited with changing the direction of reviewing which had been starting—with its sixties love of the outre—to ignore mainstream or middlebrow film. Her excitement about a then "new" director such as Steven Spielberg, or her famous profile on Cary Grant ("The Man From Dream City," July 14, 1975), are just two examples.

Despite the fact that Kael has no formal credo of her own, she is unafraid to take on "rigid" theoreticians or those whom she would consider to be academic dogmatists. Just one is aesthetician Siegfried Kracauer, whose theory of the cinema, loosely, is that it must be mimetic or depend on realism. Kael's piece on him is called "Is There A Cure For Film Criticism? Or, Some Unhappy Thoughts On Siegfried Kracauer's *Theory of Film: The Redemption of Physical Reality*" (she is famous for her clever titles that only occasionally slip into corniness, as this one does). More notorious is her diatriabe against Andrew Sarris's critical theory, "Circles and Squares: Joys and Sarris," which attacks the auteur proposition.

As disarmingly cheeky and unpretentious as Kael must have seemed at first, some have said she lost her critical objectivity in the early-1970s, when her partisan fervor destroyed her intellectual balance. What *is* unquestionably true is that her writing has more and more tended toward a similarity of tone and uniformity of ideas. In the past a reader could encounter an unexpected turn—even a sharp bring-up—in a Kael insight. But in recent years an unthrilling predictability has taken over: often her tone is one of either righteous anger or unmitigated enthusiasm. A gradual downslide to an unhappy homogeneity was first seen in *Going Steady* in 1970, in which nearly all the pieces are previously published reviews with the book being simply divided into Part One, Two, Three, etc. (*Going Steady* includes the earlier piece, "Trash, Art and the Movies," but that is the last article in a Kael collection not written for *The New Yorker,* either as a review or as one of the magazine's profile pieces. Even *The Citizen Kane Book* was originally an essay written for that magazine.)

Maybe some of the teeth were taken out of Kael's bite because she was forbidden by *The New Yorker* to comment on the work of other critics, such as her clever debunking of a Susan Sontag essay in *The Nation* about the pop pornographic *Flaming Creatures* of director Jack Smith: "I think that in treating indiscriminateness as a value, Miss Sontag has become a real swinger" ("Are Movies Going to Pieces?", the *Atlantic Monthly,* December 1964). But critics are not the only target she's lost. And this may be one major reason for her repetitiveness. In most ways, Kael's case has been won, if not by her, at least by virtue of the kind of movies that were made in the rather banal and boring 1970s. We no longer need anyone to cavil against films with ridiculously highbrow hopes, for there simply aren't that many. A call to attention for middlebrow movies, or "trash," is not necessary either, for in most instances that's all there is. And puncturing the pretentious balloon of some of the cultural overachievers of the late-1960s is no longer required: film makers, with the rest of the media, have seemingly lowered their cultural expectations of an audience. Nor is it necessary any longer to explain iconoclastic or subversive art, like the mid-career work of Robert Altman or Francis Ford Coppola or the mannerisms of purposefully jeering characters such as those Jack Nicholson chooses to play. (For Kael's piece on the "termination" of that string of characters, see

"Manic/Depressive," her review of Nicholson's *Goin' South,* in *The New Yorker,* December 11, 1978). These Kael causes have lost much of the thrill and appeal of radicalism. Similarly, it is not currently feasible to agree that the official culture is mad and popular culture not subversion but confirmation, as Kael did at a Modern Language Association convention in 1972, on a panel with Leslie Fiedler. (Fiedler, "radical" professor of English literature at the State University of New York at Buffalo and important literary critic—*Love and Death in the American Novel* is his most well-regarded book—was the first major critic to gain recognition for the study of popular culture in the academy.) It is a nice paradox that Kael—mainline detector of highbrow affectations—should find some of the more bizarre forms of film and popular culture attractive. But clearly her democratic yearnings found a home in a 1960s sensibility that once managed to synaptically merge both high and low art.

Yet curiously a "1960s sensibility" may have ironically provided a better bedrock for Gilliatt's criticism as well, although there were other reasons for the demise of her column and prose. Canons of praise for directors becoming innovatively "great" are pleasures to read, but when those same directors, such as Gilliatt's favorites Bergman and Allen, began to repeat their visions, criticism-as-praise must necessarily follow suit too. And no new masters emerged in the later years of auteurist Gilliatt's work for *The New Yorker.* It was fascinating to watch an often brilliant, foreign intellect in interesting angles to the popular culture, although once a certain experimental phase in the popular arts had ended the machinery of high-toned explanations took on the aura of cultural overkill. It's one thing to give *explications du texte* for a Beatles movie (a film like *Sgt. Pepper's Lonely Hearts Club Band,* Gilliatt observes, seems to "incarnate the free and witty rock groups" that were "clasped to the heart of an era dissident about the worth of orthodox get-ahead values") but it is quite another to liken *A Countess from Hong Kong* to *The Importance of Being Earnest.*

Film reviewing and criticism may turn out to be more wedded to time and place than any of the other arts simply by virtue of its socially reflective quality. One certain truth is that the late-1960s and early-1970s wildly encouraged the concept and practice of the critic as superstar. Autobiographical intrusions into the arts and belles lettres were widespread enough; this tendency found a perfect conjunction with an already observable trait in Kael's criticism. By the mid- to late-1960s, many culture critics like Morris Dickstein or Leslie Fiedler, taking a cue from the "new journalism," were using personal reminiscence as an integral part of their criticism, but Kael had them all beat, chronologically and hyperbolically.

In just one flashy example, she portrays herself as Katherine Hepburn's Alice Adams in "Zeitgeist and Poltergeist; Or Are Movies Going to Pieces?" in coming to worldly Los Angeles from the more refined but suddenly out-of-it San Francisco. She describes the brown and gray tweed suit she's wearing in order to make the contrast with the nearly nude bodies doing business around the pool; a perhaps overly obvious parallel with the extraordinarily different values of the two cities. A more touching reminiscence introduces Kael's review of *Shoeshine*. Recuperating from a lovers' quarrel, Kael says, she went to the film only to find out later that her estranged lover also went to the film that very night. Not that they reconciled; for life, "as *Shoeshine* demonstrates, is too complex for facile endings" ("Retrospective Reviews," *I Lost It at the Movies*). Autobiography is yet another means of showing that one has always been "in the know," too. Kael's review of Abel Gance's *Napoleon* flat out states that she and a few other clever types appreciated the recently renovated Gance decades ago in San Francisco; the fact that *Napoleon* was not shown in the properly flamboyant setting of Radio City Music Hall "back then" only shows Kael to be particularly prescient (see her *New Yorker* review of *Napoleon*, February 16, 1981).

By and large, Kael's habit of portraying herself as a particular cinematic character has abated in the past few years or so. However, Gilliatt's personal projections continue to make flattering mention mainly of the fact that she is a redhead, coyly refer to her daughter, or make a great deal of her social familiarity with the "greats" she is interviewing. If it is not "Jeanne Moreau said to me in Paris one day" it is "Diane Keaton said to me at my place in New York"; yet another day they were at "*her* apartment" [emphasis added]. Buñuel goes out to the garden of a restaurant to get her an orange because he intuits that Gilliatt, like he, will not fancy the octopus they are having for lunch. Moreau makes a paper rose for Gilliatt's daughter, Keaton brings a page for the critic from a favorite collection of rubber stamps, and so on. And sometimes it's just pure autobiography: a review of *Annie Hall*, for instance, begins "there once was a child of three with red hair who lived in a big house at the end of a long drive in a cold part of England. She had been given a toy wheelbarrow for Christmas." The comparison is with this particular "child's" self-imposed task of the removal of the stones on the drive to actor-director Woody Allen's "also redheaded" character in *Annie Hall* who "might well have embarked on a job like this." The analogy is farfetched enough, the henna hair color superfluous.

These self-aggrandizing projections seem to fall as naturally to these writers as it does for scholar-critic Dickstein in *Gates of Eden* to make cultural hay of the fact that "my wife" seemed more in touch with Bob Dylan's performance at a concert than Dickstein was, or for Andrew Sarris to pose himself as different film characters in his reviews, mentioning—albeit tongue-in-cheek—what he wore to a particular film-related event. But it surely can be said that the easy identification of critic with cinematic object, a style in synch with the autobiographical times, is ready-made for women rather eager to lose themselves in happy association with others; in the case of these two somewhat traditionally "feminine" writers, the ready concerns are (preferably) ingenue roles, or actors, to connect up with almost by appendaging.

There is no question that this type of writing seemed more at home in the golden age of the new journalism than in the more boring, banal, and retrenched last eight years or so. Which doesn't matter in Gilliatt's case since she seems to have left her film reviewing post at *The New Yorker* for good. But while Kael has generally dropped the self-serving personal analogies to actresses, she is still the controlling consciousness. A royal we-dom similar to Queen Victoria's "we are not amused" (sometimes it's Queen of Hearts' "off with their heads") has taken the place of the more flamboyant role-playing of the earlier decade. No longer are we asked to fantasize that Kael is a major cinematic character, although perhaps still a producer-director. It's not new for critics to see themselves as representatives of the audience's response, but Kael is the only one, her current criticism implies, able to ferret out the "right" response. To reject her judgment is to reject her, and who would dare? Besides, with the innundation of prose that is swirling if not circular it's extraordinarily difficult to discern and cry halt at the logical wrong turn. (In *Here at the New Yorker,* Brendan Gill suggests this illogic is due to the fact that Kael's first film reviews were aired on the radio rather than appearing in print.)

And as with any battler, when the punch was no longer necessary, much of the charm disappeared too. Like all scrappers and iconoclasts it's more fun to cat-call from the sidelines. An angry grayness has taken the place of the more technicolored thrusts and jabs of Kael's earlier, spunkier prose. Besides, not only has much of the battle been won, the reviewing format may have begun to bore Kael without her realizing it. While it certainly allows polemic, it's also easy to skirt the possibilities for disciplined argumentation (not her strongest suit in any case).

Gilliatt, who is British, began reviewing for *The New Yorker* in 1967, sharing the spot at that time with Brendan Gill. She had reviewed films (with a year off to do theater reviews) for the London *Observer* from 1961–67. Kael was asked to join the reviewing staff of *The New Yorker* in 1968, after leaving the *New Republic* in protest against the cutting of her reviews. She has said that when editor William Shawn called to ask if she would mind sharing the reviewing bill with Gilliatt, she was "busted," and "in bed with the flu." It is a wonderfully typical dramatic reportage: the job offer arriving just in time, the comic wisecrack detailing it. Kael was to be in charge of the more important six-month winter season of films, although rumor had it that she was impatient with even this arrangement. Yet the rare reference in print to the other *New Yorker* critic was always respectful. And when the 1971 film *Sunday Bloody Sunday*, for which Gilliatt had written the much-acclaimed screenplay, appeared during her reviewing cycle, Gilliatt stepped aside and Kael gave it a glowing—if clearly deserved—review.

Things went on in this stable if not even-keeled fashion for over a decade. Whereas Kael most frequently wrote lengthy pieces (her detractors accused her of logorrhea), it often seemed that Gilliatt couldn't wait to get off the critical podium and back to her fiction writing. Her pieces were not infrequently correspondingly short, bending or breaking the standard reviewing format as often as possible. So readers, even film cognoscenti, were stupefied when a March 5, 1979 *New Yorker* editorial note briefly announced that Kael had "asked for an indefinite leave of absence, to work in film production." The note explained that Kael hoped to gain some "new perspective" by participating in another branch of the industry. And the *Voice* published an article immediately declaring that Kael had gone to work with Warren Beatty in an advisory capacity, probably in production. But on June 9, 1980 her reviewing sabbatical ended as she resumed her *New Yorker* spot with a brief review of Kubrick's *The Shining*, to be followed by a second long column that took the internal workings of the industry to task. In it she discussed money men who too often are lawyers whose opinions shift as a metaphorical finger to the wind indicates a change in power. Yet they are unfortunately the ones who make the aesthetic decisions for films (the column is rhetorically titled "How Bad Are Movies, Anyway?").

Less shocking was the "resignation" of Penelope Gilliatt for "reasons of health" on May 21, 1979. In obvious emotional trouble for some time, she had had difficulty meeting deadlines and getting to screenings. (One contemporaneous interview quotes her as declaring the past ten years a personal waste.) Gilliatt's departure was spurred by a March 26 *New Yorker* profile on writer Graham Greene in which she misquoted Greene and clearly plagiarized novelist Michael Meshaw, who had written on Greene in an article for *The Nation*. Certain phrases in Gilliatt's profile were far too close to Meshaw's work on Greene to be accidental, and he wanted some acknowledgment—as well as money—from *The New Yorker*. Editor Shawn persuaded the novelist not to demand a public statement, but in a letter to *The New Statesman* Graham Greene protested being improperly quoted, and the entire matter was brought to light. Despite the furor the media made at the time (pieces appeared in *Newsweek* and the *New York Times* among other places), *The New Yorker* held firm to its policy of "no comment" and protected Gilliatt as much as possible. And while she no longer reviews films, fiction has appeared regularly since then in *The New Yorker*. *Three-Quarter Face*, a collection of Gilliatt's *New Yorker* profiles and reviews, was published to generally good reviews in the spring of 1980.

In fact, throughout her reviewing career Gilliatt wrote fiction in greater proportion to her reviews and critical articles. However, two nonfiction works were published in 1976: a book on director Jacques Tati (much of which originally appeared in *The New Yorker*) and *Jean Renoir: Essays, Conversations, and Reviews*. Gilliatt has said repeatedly that she considers herself a novelist rather than a critic, even though she was a professional reviewer in England before coming to the United States. In the introduction to *Three-Quarter Face* she openly discounts the kind of journalistic reportage that must rely only on the facts. Since most creative people only allow one a "three-quarter view" anyway, for the reporter to give a fuller picture a fictive contemplation of, almost a merging with, the subject is necessary. A good writer will unconsciously reflect the style of the object of description and, interestingly, Gilliatt spells out the method: a fuller picture is attained by "paying attention" to "small-talk, gestures, way of living," ostensibly unimportant details. Perhaps this is merely a rationale for her concentrating on the aura surrounding her subjects rather than attempting to critically "pierce the veil." It coincides with her comments in a telephone interview in New York City in February 1979 about the need for criticism to be evocative. And it surely squares with women's proverbial and perceptual abilities to latch on to the minutiae of others as a means to understanding their sensibility or their artistic "product." Gilliatt's obsession with detail is seen in much of her work, which includes the novels *The Cutting Edge, A State of Change,* and *One By One,* as well as short stories anthologized in *Splendid Lives, Nobody's Business,* and *Come Back If It Doesn't Get Better,* and *Quotations from Other Lives,* the screenplay for *Sunday Bloody Sunday,* and collaboration on an opera.

Kael is much less a woman of letters, and much more exclusively a devoted film buff. After a stint as an experimental film maker, she supported herself with odd jobs in order to have the free time to write criticism. Born in California in 1919, Kael grew up on a farm north of San Francisco. She did radio reviews as a volunteer for the station KPFA and was the manager of an art film house in Berkeley for which she wrote her now-famous program notes, eventually collected in *Kiss Kiss Bang Bang* (1968). One apocryphal story has it that the editor of a San Francisco little magazine, *City Lights,* heard Kael arguing with a friend over a film, and asked Kael to write out her argument as a review. If true, the result was Kael's first review, "Slimelight," of Chaplin's film *Limelight,* published in 1953 when she was 34. During this early period Kael also contributed to the more erudite journals such as *Film Quarterly, Sight and Sound,* the *Partisan Review,* and the *Massachusetts*

Review. Her first collection of essays and reviews, *I Lost It at the Movies* (1965), was such an extraordinary success that it propelled her out of obscurity and into the world of reviewing for national magazines.

Kiss Kiss Bang Bang was published three years later. This collection consists of a number of pieces with a fine overview, especially in the sections "Trends," "The Movies Past," and "Careers." Published originally in *The New Yorker,* "Movies on Television" is a consistently clever argument. The present and past mix randomly for Kael—and all of us— as we watch movies on TV. For Kael, this mix is the same as flying above San Francisco, where the critic had been born, gone to college, and where "now" her little daughter and dogs are waiting for her. Watching movies on television is much the same, and even better if you get up "high enough to gain the proper perspective." Unlike the other arts where a "natural selection" takes place, she observes that in movies everything is in "hopeless disorder." Good and bad films are sold together in blocks, and unfortunately that is the way "new generations experience our movies' past." Kael is a bit contradictory in not crediting the democratic selection process she usually espouses, but she passes off the difference between movies and TV by saying that while both are mass arts, TV exists solely for commercial purposes. Money men are ever the villains for the romantic Kael, and it is likely that she will come up with a similar aesthetic/moral argument regarding videodiscs.

Parenthetically, *Kiss Kiss Bang Bang* is the last Kael collection to contain cleverly nasty, and frequently ad hominem, references to other reviewers. For example, Penelope Gilliatt, in reviewing the 1961 *The Innocents,* is at "low ebb" although she is generally "the most erratically brilliant of modern critics." Writer Joan Didion, Kael's longstanding pet peeve, is attacked with particular delight in Kael's review of the film made from Didion's novel *Play It As It Lays,* even though Didion did not do the adaptation for the film. This doesn't stop Kael, however, who "whooped" with "disbelieving giggles" when she read the novel. Like a college sophomore, she "accidentally on purpose" mixes up heroines of both film and novel with Didion herself: the "ultimate princess fantasy is to be so glamorously sensitive and beautiful that you have to be taken care of; you are simply too sensitive for this world." Giving the devil her due, however, Kael admits with only some irony that "Miss Didion can write: the smoke of creation arises from those dry-ice sentences" (*The New Yorker,* November 11, 1972). The commercialism of southern California, the nihilism of European films, and any lack of moral structure, are all things that disturb Kael and that curiously Joan Didion seems to embody. *Play It As It Lays* is about the "Red Desert region of Hollywood," it's the "glamour abyss" and "lacks the moral toughness of English letters" (after all, it *is* an American work).

Kael came to New York City from San Francisco and environs at the behest of *McCall's* magazine, in order to be their regular film reviewer. She lasted only the first six months of 1966 after saying *The Sound of Music* should have been called *The Sound of Money* and wondering—with an anti-Philistinism that was clearly too much for the mainstream *McCall's*—if there wasn't perhaps "one little Von Trapp who didn't want to sing his head off, or who screamed that he wouldn't act out little glockenspiel routines for Papa's party guests, or who got nervous and threw up if he had to get on a stage? No, nothing mars this celebration of togetherness. . . . It's the big lie, the sugarcoated lie that people seem to want to eat." This is the clever kind of personalization that Kael and many women critics are so very good at; reviewing *Annie*, for instance, Kael uses it to get—as ever—the highest possible camp out of kids: "All the little orphans seem to have been trained by Ethel Merman; they belt in unison" (*The New Yorker,* May 31, 1982). Unfortunately, with *The Sound of Music*, it helped work her out of a job. Kael worked on a freelance basis for a short time, writing for *Life,* and then took Stanley Kauffmann's job for about a year at the *New Republic* until she quit in anger at the editing of her pieces. The move to *The New Yorker* came in 1968, and since then collections of *New Yorker* pieces have appeared every few years: *Going Steady* in 1970, *Deeper Into Movies* in 1973, *Reeling* in 1976, and *When the Lights Go Down* in 1980.

Titles, of course, are a Kael specialty and signature. About half of her books carry titles with the sexual double entendres that Renata Adler pointed out in her *New York Review of Books* piece. Even so, the title of *Kiss Kiss Bang Bang* might be questioned on another score. While Kael tells us in the "Note on the Title" to this 1968 collection that she saw the phrase on an Italian movie poster and it seemed to indicate the most basic appeal of movies, it's actually in anthropologist Hortense Powdermaker's 1950 classic study, *Hollywood: the Dream Factory,* that a much more ready explanation appears. Powdermaker discusses South Sea natives who have seen American movies and describe them as one of two types, either "kiss-kiss" or "bang-bang."

Although their paths to reviewing film were very different, Kael and Gilliatt share some interesting biographical similarities. Each graduated from college at an unusually early age, and each is divorced, with a daughter. Both lived on Manhattan's Upper West Side while writing for *The New Yorker,* a fact that comes up periodically in their reviews. (Recently, for reasons of health, Kael remains on her farm in western Massachusetts.) But while Kael is the product of Depression America (her father's farm shut down during the 1930s and the family moved to San Francisco), Gilliatt was the favored and privileged only child of a divorced British barrister. Upper middle class "prejudices" may tinge reviews a little less obviously than more down home ones, but Kael's tendency toward political isolationism periodically comes through. In fact, her vehemence against directors critical of America has led writer John Gregory Dunne, in an admittedly biased essay called "Pauline," to say that Kael "sniffs out fashionable anti-Americanism like a lady from the DAR."[1]

The prejudices and preferences of the two women can be readily observed in their respective reviews of a film such as Richard Lester's *Petulia* with its examination of the 1960s' love of the bizarre and its declaration that cultural dissolution is mirrored in its characters' inabilities to personally connect. Though Gilliatt got the official review in the June 15, 1968 *New Yorker*, Kael cleverly inserted her thoughts about *Petulia* in her essay "Trash, Art and the Movies." For Kael, *Petulia* with its self-concious elliptical montages is an example of pretentious art; the article is possibly the first of the notorious Kael *New Yorker* re-reviews; that is, her habit of "going over" a film she missed during her off-reviewing cycle. (And later, in the well-publicized piece on *Last Tango in Paris*, extended to prereviews as well.) There are three things Kael dislikes about *Petulia*: its jumpy editing, which puzzled many reviewers; its put-down of the America of 1968; and the cinematic uglification of Kael's favorite city-town, San Francisco. Partisan as ever, she complains that director Lester misuses filters "to destroy the city's beautiful light." (Later, the second version of *Invasion of the Body Snatchers* [1978] would be *praised* for the inversely same reason. "The story is set in San Francisco, which is the ideally right setting, because of the city's traditional hospitality to artists and eccentrics. . . . The story simply wouldn't be as funny in New York City, where people are not so relaxed, or so receptive to new visions" *The New Yorker*, December 25, 1978).

Kael, rejecting *Petulia*'s cross-cutting, which tried to connect up the personal and the political and calling the film a "jagged glittering mosaic" that uses unsuccessful "little montages," reserves her real vigor for what she terms the director's "Hate Letter to America." Here is the crux of the matter, and the one Kael canon that remains fixed, for although the concepts of "honor" and "good and bad" come up repeatedly in her writing the morality is completely her own and shifts at will. She cannot bear highbrow aspirations. Her hatred of elitist values allows her to attack where others fear to tread, as in her pioneer criticisms of Bergman, Antonioni, and Fellini. But it also forces her out onto some precarious critical limbs, as when she tries to make a doctrine for Spielberg's films, or says that sometimes bad movies are more important than good ones ("So Off-Beat We Lose the Beat"). Or when she claims—with a bias that turns to illogic—that in *Petulia* "the few good ideas don't really shine as they do in simpler trash." Still, because she is such a clever writer, when Kael calls Lester a "cinemagician," it does seem appallingly, damningly, right. Although she bandages the wound by saying that "Lester should trust himself more as a director . . . because there's good, tense direction in a few sequences," Kael would just as soon remake Lester's direction by stripping away all the stylistic frippery and getting right to the melodramatic or populist heart of the matter.

For Gilliatt, style is significant because it provides metaphorical and metaphysical possibilities, her specialties. Instead of disparaging Julie Christie's role—a wealthy playboy's wife toying with the affections of a surgeon played by George C. Scott—as a spoiled "kook" as Kael might, Gilliatt perceives that Petulia's irrepressible and irresponsible mannerisms could be a cover for her sensitivity to a world that is, in its self-conscious 1960s modernity, fragilely impermanent. Gilliatt probes: "the girl re-designs reality by quirkiness and by living without a sense of consequence. She breaks up the structure constantly, so that it is smashed before she has had time to grow fond of it or to see someone else's boot destroy it." And Gilliatt can zero in on one frame or shot and find, as would an early semiologist, the meaning of the film. In speaking of the two main characters' tendency to purposefully immunize themselves against the pain of life she decides the effect is that of a "frame of sterile cloths lapped around an operating incision point, which allows a surgeon to forget that surgery hurts: this Mondrian square of skin obviously has nothing much in common with the body he saw in his own bathroom mirror the same morning. The cloths stylize the act of cutting so that it hardly seems related to wounding. . . . Lester's two characters stylize what happens to them by the same necessity, in case it should turn out to be a gash in their own flesh." Full use is made of surgical metaphors.

By treating just the three main characters of *Petulia* and concentrating on only the film's emotional impact, Gilliatt completely omits any references to the sociological and political connections that drive Kael mad. Kael, on the other hand, ignores the emotional hit of *Petulia* to make her main point: that we're *not* all guilty, rich, violent, spoiled, and so on. At least, not Kael. Gilliatt's imaginative, fictionlike, rendering of a film can lead her to some fabulously farfetched comparisons. She compares the emotional layering of *Petulia* to Chekhov: "something quite else is always going on beneath the self-protectiveness and backchat, something aching, as it does in Carlotta's lines while she is doing her magic turns in *The Cherry Orchard.*" But Chekhov is a perhaps too frequently used standard of comparison in Gilliatt's reviews. She often names the great Russian dramatist when he doesn't necessarily apply; that is, he *might*, but another reference could work as well. Not only does *The Cherry Orchard*'s Carlotta serve for Petulia, she is also the analogy for Maureen Stapleton's Pearl in *Interiors* (both Carlotta and Pearl could do card tricks; both might be "tenderly" called vulgarians).

Predictably, Gilliatt admired Woody Allen's *Interiors* tremendously in her August 7, 1978 review. Her affinity for Allen and Diane Keaton is more than obvious. (See particularly Gilliatt's profile of Keaton, "Her Own Best Disputant," *The New Yorker,* December 25, 1978). In fact, Allen and *The New Yorker* seem to have a nice reciprocal relationship in general. His satirical pieces have been published there, he is mentioned in "Goings On About Town" every week for saxophone playing at Michael's Pub, and although the magazine rarely advertises films, there were full-page ads for *Interiors* run throughout 1978. Naturally Allen returns the compliment. In the film, his heroine Renata has been published in *The New Yorker,* the highest accolade for a poet, *Interiors* is proud to announce.

Possibly Gilliatt's love affair with Allen's films and troupe has most to do with a perfect blend of subject matter and interpretive method. Gilliatt, like some updated metaphysical poet, is terribly good at deriving the meaning of the whole from the specific detail of a film. Here women's finely-tuned abilities with detail seem to pass into the realm of intense intellectual embroidery, and Allen's work, particularly in *Interiors,* yields the precise type of minutiae Gilliatt likes to focus on. "Near the beginning," she reports, "there is a close-up of Diane Keaton's profile and her hand on a windowpane, the fingers stretching for a freedom that her life has not afforded her." Perhaps. While true to her own class bias, a Kael might ask what other possible economic, social, and professional freedoms a woman of Renata's class could require. Gilliatt finds other visually symbolic parallels: "Near the beginning, too, there is a held shot of the back of E.G. Marshall's head as he stares out of a window." The analogy is carried through (or forced): "All the characters in this film look at the world as if it were partitioned off from them, as if it were separated from them by something as transparent as glass, and as unbreakable by people in control of themselves."

Yet it is downright painful to watch Gilliatt do metaphysical somersaults in making much over the intellectual possibilities of a film like Allen's *Everything You Always Wanted To Know About Sex.* After a lengthy description of the sketches that make up the film (the main one—of the body as Central Control—is not as original as she assumes, having been used first by Sid Caesar in an early "Your Show of Shows"), she pompously concludes that the film "seems to relate to the whole immensely solemn body of American literature about male impotence and dither, which in turn has given rise to hundreds of Broadway and Hollywood comedies." Gilliatt does not have complete critical blinders on, however, and it is a relief to see that her review of *Bananas* finds parts of the film "lame."

It may be safely said that Gilliatt's considerable abilities with metaphor and image are what she leans on the most in reviews packed disproportionately with description. A similar visual detailing of characters can be observed in her fiction. In her short story "As We Have Learned from Freud, There Are No Jokes," a character is described as having a face "so asymmetrical that a reflection of it in a piece of broken mirror on the wall was unrecognizable" (*Nobody's Business*, 1972).

Interiors fortunately affords many such moments to describe and "evoke." Gilliatt settles on a scene in New York's St. Patrick's Cathedral when Eve (Geraldine Page) realizes that her husband Arthur (Edward G. Marshall) really *is* going to leave her for another woman: "In one of the very few violent scenes in this stilled, attentive film, she sweeps her arm across a row of burning votive candles in the church and runs shouting up the aisle." (They have stopped in to get away from the crowds on Fifth Avenue to have a quiet chat.) But Gilliatt in her partisanship ignores any possible flaws of the film. In fact she hyperbolically declares *Interiors* to be as "true a tragedy as any that has come out of America in my memory. The end of the story speaks about parenthood as clearly as King Lear." She makes as little as possible of the obviously Bergman-derived qualities of the film, which nearly every critic noted, but she does add that many "quick cuts" (editing) of the film are "entirely original." And once again she concludes that the "theme its characters express is very Chekhovian."

Gilliatt's review appeared in the August 7, 1978 *New Yorker* when the film opened. But upon her annual autumnal reappearance, Pauline Kael proceeded to re-review the film. Clearly she felt it important enough to warrant a Kael commentary. In a twelve-page round-up review and state-of-the-art essay, provocatively entitled "Fear of Movies" (September 25, 1978), Kael reviews all the films she didn't get a crack at while she was "off" her cycle.

Her tendency to place the director into the film can be observed in her overview of *Interiors*, a mini-piece included in "Fear of Movies." Employing psychobiography with a very broad brush, Kael decides the basic "problem" of the film is a Jewish one. Here she ignores the fact that the film's subject is an upper-middle-class WASP family and that there are no Semitic characters at all. Since Woody Allen is Jewish, Kael declares *Interiors* to be "the ultimate Jewish movie." She queries if we are "expected to ask ourselves who in the movie is Jewish and who Gentile? . . . Surely at root the family problem is Jewish: it's not the culture in general that imposes the humanly impossible standards of achievement—they're a result of the Jewish fear of poverty and persecution and the Jewish reverence for learning. It's not the joy of making cinema that spurs Woody Allen on (as he made clear in *Annie Hall*, he can't have that kind of joy), it's the discipline of making cinema."

For Kael, Allen—actor, director, public personality—is the central character in the film, although he is unseen, or unrealized, by the rest of us. Criticism by personal fiat can never fail, and of course it seems brilliantly original since only the critic sees the character around whom conjectures and connections fly. It works particularly well for movies, since frequently publicity has preceded criticism in letting us know a great deal about the film's personnel. Gilliatt, for example, ends her review of Fassbinder's *The Bitter Tears of Petra von Kant* with a less intrusive but still cheaply Freudian observation about the director: "one remembers that he ran away from home himself at sixteen." Woody Allen is ideal for this approach, since he is so often the central character. Significantly, however, not in *Interiors,* where for Kael the two mothers in the film are the two sides of the Jewish matriarch warring for control of Woody Allen: "the first (the real mother) clearly has him in the stronger grip. She represents the death of the instinct, but she also represents art, or at least cultivation and pseudo-art." Even when regarding Allen's work in toto, as Kael does in her October 27, 1980 review-essay on *Stardust Memories* where she treats mainly *Annie Hall* and *Manhattan,* the films seem to be solely about Allen's relationship with his Jewishness. But, clearly, this is *not* the only theme of the film, as myriad other pieces—like Joan Didion's in the July 7, 1979 *New York Review of Books*—amply demonstrate.

In "Fear of Movies," as well as in discussing *Interiors,* Kael continues her ongoing argument in favor of the use of violence in films. It is a diatribe begun ten years earlier in a *New Yorker* review of *Bonnie and Clyde,* although in 1978 the onus is completely on the public. Kael declares that people avoid "upsetting" (or subversive, or great, or violent) art because they are afraid, not because they have good taste. A case in point is Kael's favorite Sam Peckinpah, whose recent offering, *Convoy,* didn't do well at the box office possibly because the public is "punishing" Peckinpah for forcing violence upon it in the past. Again the metaphorical rights and wrongs, the angers to be alleviated or dispelled, here projected upon the movie audience (and for all the querulousness with Andrew Sarris, promulgator of the directorial theory in the United States, the assumption is an auteurist one).

A piece written only two years earlier, "Notes on the Nihilistic Poetry of Sam Peckinpah," is more even-handed, albeit unashamedly partisan, in assessing the director's obsession with violence. He's "lost a lot of blood" with his "long history of butchered films" and so "the bedevilled bastard's got a right to crow." It's understandable to Kael, who's known him for over ten years, though recently his "vision has become so scabrous, theatrical, and obsessive that it is now controlling him."

It's one thing to analyze a director's film according to his "vision," quite another to merge the person and the movie. It's a type of "montage-criticism" that Kael applies at will, particularly when she is the most worked up. The movie under review here is *The Killer Elite*, and is "about selling yourself yet trying to hang on to a piece of yourself. Peckinpah turned 50 while he was preparing this picture, and, what with booze, illnesses, and a mean, self-destructive streak, in recent years he has looked as if his body were giving out. This picture is about survival." Kael slides from film to director back to film as if Peckinpah were physically in the movie. Everything melds together in a wonderful descriptive wash.

Kael's tendency toward verbal pile-up has increased with time, as the more subtly argumentative earlier essay on *Bonnie and Clyde*—also an apologia for violence—shows. Although she is basing her argument on the recurring notion that it is "generally *only* good movies that provoke attacks," this time she is in the service of the legal right of film makers to use violence and so it is nearly a moral right for the director to rub our noses in the violence, to make us uncomfortable (what good liberal would disagree here?). Kael is functioning as a cheerfully lowbrow Herbert Marcuse, but it is important for us to remember the furor that surrounded some of the more blood-spatteringly explosive scenes in *Bonnie and Clyde*.

We're naturally more accustomed to the free intermingling of personal and cinematic details when an actor is the entire subject of a critical piece. And while a highly personal response from the writer is much less of a shock (one thinks of the self-confessed infatuations of James Agee with certain actresses), Kael still manages to be charmingly extreme in her enthusiasms, if sometimes too close to fanzine jargon. In her much-touted profile on Cary Grant, "The Man From Dream City," Kael personalizes, "If the roof leaks, or the car stalls, or you don't know how to get the super to keep his paws off you, you may long for a Clark Gable to take charge, but when you think of going out, Cary Grant is your dream date—not sexless but sex with civilized grace, sex with mystery. He's the man of the big city, triumphantly sun-tanned." (*The New Yorker*, July 14, 1975) A conglomerate view and knowledge of all Grant's films and roles are assumed.

Male critics, of course, have written as eloquently in pieces that erase the demarcation between actor and role (an Otis Ferguson article on James Cagney is one, Bazin's piece on the personal implications of Chaplin's *Limelight* is another), and that see the work on an actor as ouevre. But women critics in general, not just Kael and Gilliatt, as ostentatious as they are in their predilections, seem happy to posit a conscious or willed quality in the actor's selection of certain parts. It is easy to suggest that women are traditionally more willing to lend mythic proportions and power to others; it is a curiously nice fit with the cinema, which nearly *sui generis* grants myth. Kael is not unaware, of course, of this property, and even prophesies its increasing importance: "the whole area of screen acting is probably going to be a big can of worms in the next few years. We are already looking for closer identity between actor and role in many movies. . . . We never had the slightest illusion we were seeing Doris Day as she was offscreen, and that hardly concerned us. In the kind of acting now being required, it does concern us . . . mainly because of a new interest in less structured and less stereotyped approaches to character than in past movies." ("Waiting for Orgy," a review of *Bob and Carol and Ted and Alice, The New Yorker,* October 4, 1969)

Yet Kael's particularly personal reactions to actors have become more extreme with time—emotional, visceral, even sexual—as her well publicized review of Bertolucci's *Last Tango in Paris* shows in discussing Brando: "His first sex act has a boldness that had the audience gasping and the gasp was caused—in part—by our awareness that this was Marlon Brando doing it, not an unknown actor. . . . We are watching *Brando* throughout this movie, with all the feedback that that implies . . . if Brando knows this hell, why should we pretend we don't-? . . . [for] . . . We all know that movie actors often merge with their roles in a way that stage actors don't, quite." (*The New Yorker,* October 28, 1972)

Though not nearly so proclamatory, Gilliatt similarly melds individual artist with role. Discussing Woody Allen's *Love and Death,* for example, she decides that the "vividly alert Diane Keaton is one of the few witty women in public life so far who have managed also to be clowns without feeling unconsciously bound to mock themslves" (*The New Yorker,* June 14, 1975). But she does not consider her subject as paradigmatic of a particular stage in American cultural history as Kael does. In "Marlon Brando: An American Hero," Kael observes that in very early films such as *The Wild One* and *On the Waterfront,* Brando was our "new primitive, a Byronic Dead End Kid, with his quality of vulnerability." If he later parodies himself in a film like *Sayonara* (1957) or *Morituri* (1965) it is because like "many another great actor who has become fortune's fool, he plays the great ham, for Brando's *career* is a larger demonstration of the same principle at work in mass culture; but instead of becoming moral, he (like Norman Mailer) became an eccentric, which in this country means a clown, possibly the only way left to preserve some kind of difference." He becomes a "buffoon," which, in America, is the fate of all "our Hamlets." (Another example Kael provides, though an undeveloped one, is John Barrymore, who also had to choose the path of eccentricity.) While it sounds like a cultural declaration with the force of morality behind it, it's really just a suggestion.

Then the summation, in typical fashion neither explained nor supported, which passes for intellect but may be just flourishes: "Perhaps Brando has been driven to this self-parody so soon because of his imaginative strength and because of that magnetism that makes him so compelling an expression of American conflicts." But we are not told just what those conflicts are.

One might say that Kael is free-wheeling, or ruthless, in combining facts "about" an actor with an interpretation of the part *cum* bits and pieces about America in order to come up with her four-and-twenty blackbirds of a cultural pie with an actor in the middle; at least she did this from the very start. In her first film review—Charlie Chaplin's 1952 film *Limelight*—she criticizes the actor's performance because "the egotism of his self-revelation has infected the tragic beauty." And besides, audiences may be responding negatively because they've caught on to the fact that he is not a "regular fellow" and has been too much the artist ("Slimelight," *City Lights,* no. 3, 1953).

Whether or not critics are pop personalities, Kael is as passionate and intrusive in discussing them, and in introducing subtle biographical details. An essay on Siegfried Kracauer, the major film theoretician whose work is based on materialistic realism, is nastily, wittily entitled "Is There A Cure For Film Criticism? Or, Some Unhappy Thoughts on Siegfried Kracauer's *Theory of Film: The Redemption of Physical Reality.*" Kael complains that Kracauer is the type of critic who can't appreciate a lovely day without first telling us what a day is, etc., etc., so that our enthusiasm for his favorite films is destroyed. "It is always said of George Lukacs that his best stuff isn't in English" Kael observes, "Kracauer's best stuff isn't in English either." Conceding that "a man who likes Fred Astaire can't be all pedant," she goes on to explain that "he's like a man trying to sneak his dear—but naughty—friends into Heaven." (Rigid theory and dogma are anathema to Kael, so it's no surprise that she thinks that the more "single-minded and dedicated to untenable propositions the theorist is, the more likely he is to be regarded as serious and important and 'deep'—in contrast to relaxed men of good sense whose pluralistic approaches can be disregarded as not fundamental enough." Naturally Kael's own work fits this last description perfectly.)

Kael was not afraid to take on Kracauer's classic of film scholarship, *From Caligari to Hitler* (a landmark, she says, only in the sense that "nobody else has done anything like it, Gott se dank!") nor—even more significantly from the point of view of popular acceptance—the auteur theory of Andrew Sarris, which was growing apace in both high and low critical circles. Of course it was just this iconoclasm of Kael's—a tiny, elfin-like lady from San Francisco as Giant Killer slaying all the Eastern establishment critical types—that got her national attention.

The most famous of these dissenting essays is "Circles and Squares: Joys and Sarris." Primary promoter of the auteur theory in the United States (and now film critic for the *Village Voice* and professor of film studies at Columbia University), Sarris picked up from the film criticism of Godard, Truffaut, and other "nouvelle vague" 1950s film makers in France the importance of the directorial vision. The ascending criteria for being called auteur as Sarris saw it was the technical competence of the director, his distinguishable personality, and ultimately the "tension" between the director's personality and the material. Although Sarris is commonly credited with the definition of the auteur theory, one may make a case, as an examination of very early film criticism by women shows, for earlier discovery of the theory.

Kael uses standard argumentative tricks such as finding exceptions to Sarris's categories, or reducing his logical syllogisms ad absurdum. She is particularly good at this. If "the distinguishable personaltiy of the director" is a criterion of value, then "the smell of a skunk is more distinguishable than the perfume of a rose; does that make it better?" But Sarris himself is not left out either: his critical language is "barbarous." While a film critic need not be a theoretician, Kael declares, it is "necessary that he knows how to use words. This might, indeed, be a first premise for a theory." The main objection to the theory proper is that we're committed to defending the absolute worst of a great director's films and to ignoring the perhaps very fine work of an unknown. For Kael, a "'good' critic helps people understand a work, while a 'great' one is passionately able to excite people so they will want to experience more of the art already there." Of course it was this tempest in the tiny if temperamental teapot of critical controversy that brought media light to Kael, at that time still living in California.

Probably Kael's most (in)famous critical ploy to date was her "pre-review" of Altman's 1975 film *Nashville*, which she wrote before the final version was ready. Loyalty to Altman here translated for some into the work of a publicist, and the piece so infuriated Vincent Canby that he devoted a Sunday *Times* think piece to his thoughts on the practice, calling it "On Reviewing Films Before They're Finished." "If," the *Times* chief film reviewer wonders, "one can review a film on the basis of an approximately three-hour rough-cut, why not review it on the basis of a five-hour rough-cut? A ten-hour cut? On the basis of the screenplay? The original material if first printed as a book? On the basis of press releases? Gossip items?" (March 9, 1975) Kael's overwhelmingly positive review was used for promotion purposes for the movie in the same way United Artists reprinted her review of *Last Tango in Paris* in its entirety.

Kael's disclaimer, however, is that "*Nashville* isn't in its final shape yet, and all I can do is suggest something of its achievement." She nicely explains its structure: "The picture is at once a Grand Hotel-style narrative, with twenty-four linked characters; a country-and-Western musical; a documentary essay on Nashville and American life; a meditation on the love affair between performers and audiences; and an Altman party." But the primary analogy is to James Joyce and his complex masterwork *Ulysses:* "Altman, from a Catholic background, has what Joyce had: a love of the supreme juices of everyday life. He can put unhappy characters on the screen (Keenan Wynn plays a man who loses the wife he's devoted to) and you don't wish you didn't have to watch them; you accept their unhappiness as a piece of the day, as you do in *Ulysses.*" Kael is generally unabashed by such extreme analogies—unexplained here except for the Catholic commonality and shared stream-of-consciousness, neither of which are terribly well worked-through—and that rely in part on the biographical off-chance that Altman too is Catholic.

Many have observed that reviewing—with daily, weekly, or even monthly deadlines—entails pressures that paradoxically stultify, hence hyperbole is the not infrequent result as a last-ditch, desperate rhetorical reach. Yet this need not be; one can observe some more subtle differentiations in John Simon's review and explanation of the same film in his *Esquire* piece on *Nashville* in which he offers the same analogy. There are "more or less interconnected, self-important but essentially humdrum lives strutting in a brief time span against the more important backdrop of an exceptionally raucous but second-rate city, and the whole thing functioning on two levels. But there are two sizable differences: the non-literal level in the book [*Ulysses*] is mythic, not merely allegorical, and the novel is a work of genius, the film only of talent" (September, 1975).

By contrast, Kael rather sloppily, if eliptically and "cinematically," projects (in apology for Altman's intellectual awkwardness in interviews), "if pinned to the wall by publicity men, how would Joyce have explained the "Nighttown" sequence of *Ulysses?*" Most important, "I've never before seen a movie I loved in quite this way: I sat there smiling at the screen, in complete happiness. It's a pure emotional high, and you don't come down when the picture is over; you take it with you." Kael generally goes for the spirited risk taker and this is one way she has in the past explained Altman's schizophrenic relationship with success: "Robert Altman is almost frighteningly nonrepetitive. He goes out in a new direction each time, and he scores an astonishing fifty percent—one on, one off. *M*A*S*H* was followed by *Brewster McCloud,* and *McCabe and Mrs. Miller* has now been followed by *Images.* I can hardly wait for his next movie" (*The New Yorker,* December 23, 1972). Partisanship does not always cloud her critical vision, of course, as the mildly satirical conclusion above shows, and of course she panned two

Altman films in a row: *A Wedding* (1978) and *Quintet* (1979).

Aside from the *Nashville* piece, Kael's most notorious reviewing splash has probably been her review of *Last Tango in Paris*, which was reprinted without commentary as a full-page ad in the *New York Times* and caused many an intellectual-elitist to snicker up his or her sleeve. She began her review in the strongest terms imaginable: "Bernardo Bertolucci's *Last Tango in Paris* was presented for the first time on the opening night of the New York Film Festival, October 14, 1972; that date should become a landmark in movie history comparable to May 28, 1913—the night *Le Sacre du Printemps* was first performed in music history." And there have been a number of complaints that her eagerness runs to promotional puff pieces. In an article in *Take One*, the Canadian film magazine, Mitch Tuchman gauges that the "alarming change" in Kael occurred on November 13, 1971, with her review of *Fiddler on the Roof*, after which began her progression "from scourge of the film industry to saviour" (November, 1977). It is true that some of her writing has taken on the tone of *Variety* reporting. Her review of Martin Brest's *Hot Tomorrows*, which actually was shown in the fall 1977 New York Film Festival, gets a mention in a late 1978 *New Yorker* because the film happened to be appearing in a retrospective, "American Mavericks," at a small New York theater. The name of the theater is even mentioned within the review, along with the precise financial details surrounding the film's deals. Some feel that Kael "calmed down" after the Adler attack, and that in the past few years her pieces have been more moderate in tone.

But her enthusiasm, while tending toward heavy overstatement, is perhaps Kael's best quality. And when she puts it to the service of a new talent, she's at her messianic best: excited, ingenuous, and vitally descriptive. Her review of Martin Scorcese's 1973 film *Mean Streets*, for instance, did much to establish a young director's first major work, and is a piece of writing that can still stand as a perfect running description of the opening sequence of the film: "It has its own unsettling, episodic rhythm and a high-charged emotional range that is dizzyingly sensual. At the beginning, there's a long, fluid sequence as the central character, Charlie, comes into a bar and greets his friends; there's the laying on of hands, and we know that he is doing what he always does. And when the camera glides along with him as he's drawn toward the topless dancer on a barroom stage, we share his trance." ("Everyday Inferno," *The New Yorker,* October 8, 1973) Too, she "rescued" Altman's *McCabe and Mrs. Miller* from a mixed critical reception and probable oblivion by giving it a review that captured the film's elegiac charm ("Pipe Dream," *The New Yorker,* July 3, 1971). Other reviewers then joined in; one— Arthur Knight of *Saturday Review*—even went so far as to say: "Influenced in part by Pauline Kael's glowing account of the film in a recent

New Yorker . . . I recently saw *McCabe and Mrs. Miller* again. . . . And it was like seeing another movie!" (July 24, 1971).

If Kael is a romantic in her pioneering, energetic discoveries of "new talent," Gilliatt is a classicist in her limning of certain great directors and favorites. Her two books of criticism (aside from the collections of reviews in *Unholy Fools* and *Three-Quarter Face*) are both worshipful accounts of directors. *Tati* (1976) is not much more probing than a long essay on comedian Jacques Tati that begins rather preciously: "Jacques Tati, onlie begetter of Monsieur Hulot, is the one film comedian today who is Keaton's equal." And there is a reverent collection of "Essays, Conversations, Reviews," subtitle of a book simply titled *Jean Renoir* (1975), as well as admiring *New Yorker* profiles on director Luis Buñuel, French film archivist Henri Langlois, an adoring piece on Jeanne Moreau in *Three-Quarter Face* (although the ill-fated plagiarized essay on Graham Greene has been omitted). Of course the critic defends herself in advance by admitting that her work on Renoir, for example, is not "distantly analytic: his work forbids distance, since it invites you into his company, like great music or Chekhov. [!] His work is eloquent enough to talk for itself, and so is he." And, as to the "lack of analysis proper, I can only think of something Renoir once said to me on the subject, with his usual absence of asperity: 'There is a certain type of person who wonders if it is the eggs on the muffin that makes eggs Benedict.'" This is the kind of dismissal of criticism that one encounters in self-consciously anti-intellectual circles, or in undergraduate, generally sophomore literature courses. And an odd fence for an elitist critic—particularly one writing for *New Yorker* readers—to straddle.

But it is an artlessness that allows Gilliatt to be more open to an "amoral" modern sensibility than the other *New Yorker* critic (although ironically, Kael—the critic who's still there—may turn out to be more in line with a less chic, more standard sense of propriety). The most obvious example is Gilliatt's extraordinary screenplay for John Schlesinger's *Sunday Bloody Sunday* (1971). Not only is the "new" morality of a threesome with a bisexual man as fulcrum explored, but so is the dissatisfaction of the woman, rather than the "other man," with the "sharing" set-up (a prescient pitch in the direction of women's more openly expressed emotional and sexual demands). It is Alex (Glenda Jackson) who declares: "I've had this business that anything is better than nothing. There are times when nothing *has* to be better than anything." Nor is Gilliatt—in her criticism—disturbed by the nihilism of an Antonioni or a Fassbinder (see particularly her reviews of *The Passenger* and *The Bitter Tears of Petra von Kant*). At the very least, she is never less than sophisticated.

By contrast, Kael's ideas often seem reactionary. Though her response might be seen as a refreshing one, she gave one of the few negative reviews to the smugly feminist Agnes Vardas film *One Sings, the Other Doesn't* (1977), by unforgivably titling it "Scrambled Eggs." According to the film, says Kael, "the purpose of sex in this movie seems to be to have an abortion. That's the real high. Abortion is the new rite of passage to be reported to one's friends with sad pride.... Charming young girls setting their belligerent jaws and singing about their ovules." But less successfully satirical, and more openly emotional ... and nasty: "when her husband expects her [Pomme, the film's heroine, played by Valerie Mairesse] to prepare dinner—an activity that would conflict with her creative thinking about a new song" (*The New Yorker,* November 14, 1977). Misogyny, not just hatred of bad movies, too frequently comes through. Of *Wanda,* director Barbara Loden's film about an "ordinary" woman who leaves her kids with her ex-husband and runs off with an unsavory character, Kael declares: "We've all known dumb girls, and we've all known unhappy girls; the same girls are not often, I think, both dumb and unhappy. Wanda is a double depressant—a real stringy-haired ragmop" (March 20, 1971). Lina Wertmuller's 1975 film *Seven Beauties* is reviewed in *The New Yorker* as *Seven Fatties.*

It's generally open season on other women writers, as we have seen in the case of Sontag and Didion though—slippery as ever—Kael complains about Mary McCarthy on these very grounds. Kael's essay "The Making of *The Group*" points out that McCarthy "always satirized women." It is, Kael condescends though being somewhat mea culpa-ish about it, "a terrible feminine weakness—our coquettish way of ridiculing ourselves, hoping perhaps that we can thus be accepted as feminine ... We try to protect ourselves as women by betraying other women." (Yet she can be quite acceptably "feminist" when it suits her: a euology for Mae Marsh declares that what made Marsh so terrific, even as a star of the "silent screen," were her realistic, human attributes, which do not depend on a mythologized chivalric double standard. She uses Lillian Gish for comparative purposes. Gish is "pure and fluid and lilylike," but her "idealized feminity" can make her seem "rather neurotic and frightening." Whereas Marsh is "less ethereal," "less actressy," a "sensual, ordinary woman." She is our dream "not of heavenly beauty, like Gish, but of earthly beauty." (*The New Yorker,* February 24, 1978)

However, it's not just women that come under attack. Hypocritical liberals are a particular bête noir, as we see in Kael's conclusion to her review of *Hud:* "they are split, and it shows in a million ways. I imagine they're very like the people who made *Hud,* and like them they do rather well for themselves. They're so careful to play the game at their jobs that if they hadn't told you that they're *really* screwing the system, you'd never guess it." ("Hud, Deep in the Divided Heart of Hollywood") Her essay, "The Come-Dressed-As-the-Sick-Soul-of-Europe-Parties" was immediate in 1961 in making fun of Antonioni's *La Notte,* Resnais's *Last Year at Marienbad,* and Fellini's *La Dolce Vita.* These nihilistic films show "the last gasp of depleted academia;" the rhetorical question is are they "new and deep" or more likely "simply empty?" Besides—and here Kael tips her hand—"if the malaise affects only the rich, is it so very important?" (Both pieces are collected in *I Lost It at the Movies.*)

One major exception to Kael's antipathy toward the Europeans is her admiration for Truffaut's *Jules and Jim.* Particularly because Jeanne Moreau's Catherine has "despite her need to intrude and dominate, the gift for life. She holds nothing in reserve; she lives out her desires; when she can't control the situation, she destroys it. Catherine may be wrong-headed, as those who aspire to be free spirits often are (and they make this wrongness more visible than pliable, amiable people do), but she is devoid of hypocrisy and she doesn't lie." (1961, "Jules and Jim," *I Lost It at the Movies*). Kael is moralizing here as usual, but it's the high-handedness of the romatic egoist that she so clearly admires about Catherine: a quality that she as a critic possesses. And one that has gotten her into a lot of hot water.

A famous ploy along these lines was Kael's attempt to blow the lid off the reputation of Orson Welles' generally acclaimed masterpiece *Citizen Kane* in her 1971 book—really a long introduction to the shooting script—*Raising Kane: The Citizen Kane Book*—which was first published in *The New Yorker.* Yet some would claim that her rather flashy presentation was not only foolhardy but, unlike Truffaut's Catherine, duplicitous as well. Kael's goal here was to transfer the credit for the film to screenwriter Herman Mankiewicz and to debunk Welles's reputation as a genius.

According to Kael, she had a contract with Bantam Books to write an introduction for an edition of the shooting script for *Citizen Kane.* Bit by bit, the project got longer until finally she took it to *New Yorker* editor William Shawn who became interested in publishing it: great publicity for the eventual sale of the book. Although she was originally given only $750 for the Bantam introduction, Kael reportedly received $50,000 from *The New Yorker.*

That's one simple and straightforward explanation of the book. Yet according to Professor Howard Suber of UCLA's Graduate School of Cinema and Critical Studies, he held a contract to do a book on the shooting script at the same time Kael did. His contract was with another New York publisher, Dutton, and Bantam outbid Dutton. As a result, Kael contacted Suber in California, offering to share royalties as well as kudos and asking him to write an essay to be included in her book. Suber had done extensive work on the filmscripts, and the members of his graduate seminar on *Citizen Kane* had undertaken original research. One of the "finds" was that a member of his class was a stepchild of Dorothy Comingore, Kane's Susan in the film, who had been in a sanatorium for awhile, and at that time—in the early 1970s—was married to a mailman in Connecticut. The class scraped together the bus fare for Comingore to come out to Los Angeles to talk to the class.

Later, Kael flew to Hollywood and heard the findings of the class. Yet, the book's introduction implies that *Kael* "discovered" Comingore, a bit player: "Dorothy Comingore says, 'When I read for Orson, Herman was in the room, with a broken leg and a crutch, and Orson turned to him and said, 'What do you think?' and Herman said, 'Yes, she looks precisely like the image of a kitten we've been looking for.'" Suber also believes that he was the first to point out to Kael that no one is there to hear Kane's voice say "Rosebud" at the end of the film. In the book she says, "I noticed once again, though without being bothered by it this time, either, that there was no one in the room to hear the dying Kane say "Rosebud." Later Kael sent Suber a check for $350, which he cashed, and that—from her point of view if not his—was that. While Suber may be just another disgruntled academic critic, Kael obviously should have made some mention of his and his class's contribution.[2]

Some of Welles's reputation for creative input and for being not entirely ungrateful for Mankiewicz's contribution has been at least partially restored by Peter Bogdanovich's article "The Kane Mutiny" that recounts Suber's "side," as well (*Esquire*, October 1972). And the final decision on the precise proportion of script input from both Mankiewicz and Welles seems to be in: a comprehensive article by Robert Carringer in the winter 1978 *Critical Inquiry* examines all the scripts of *Citizen Kane*. Welles's writing style and revision methods are clearly in the filmscripts; so is his bold use of montage and his personal concept of Charles Foster Kane. But whatever accusations were made about Kael, the "new" attention focused on the screenwriter (and away from the director) came from a Kael Putsch and gained momentum from her book. She also insists that cinematographer Gregg Toland should get more credit for the visual innovations of *Citizen Kane*. Kael found a 1935 German film, *Mad Love*, which Toland shot and which used not only the image of a cockatoo much in the way *Citizen Kane* did, but also some stylized shots of *Mad Love*'s hero, Peter Lorre, similar to the placement of Welles's Kane. This leads Kael to conclude that some of the gothic angles and shadows, and the famous high ceilings and big rooms, must also be owing to Toland's style, learned at the directorial knee of German expressionist Karl Freund. Therefore he is "responsible by affecting the conception."

Still, with Kael's flair for controversy, *The Citizen Kane Book* in its own way is a minor classic, albeit earning the sub rosa title *The Citizen Kael Book*. And in her work on Kane, many major trends of Kael's criticism are present: the uplifting of a slighted or wronged figure, the reapportionment of credit as Kael feels it should be distributed, the brilliant if somewhat superficial and perhaps not-too-well-researched insight. And she doesn't miss the opportunity to define *Citizen Kane* as "kitsch reclaimed." It is "Freud plus scandal, a comic strip about Hearst." Kael emphasizes the spontaneous "accidental" character of the cinema—that a good movie is not necessarily pre-planned and therefore is not really the work solely of the director; rather it is "a superb example of collaboration." Moreover, Kael's personal intervention—nearly divination—is required. When searching for a link, "I looked up his credits as a cameraman . . . I closed my eyes and visualized it, and there was the gothic atmosphere," etc.

In her reviews, Kael has frequently called attention not just to the screenwriter, so often overlooked in this auteur-oriented world, but to other contributors as well. She was one of the first, happily, to pinpoint editor Dede Allen's work, giving it early recognition in the widely anthologized 1967 review of *Bonnie and Clyde*. But the recurrent motif is the constant pressing for the narrative and literary elements of film. The importance of Herman Mankiewicz's script is just one example, but her literary bent can be seen in her other writing too. "What must it be like," she queries in her review of Peter Davis's documentary on Vietman, *Hearts and Minds,* "for those who know and love only movies, and not literature as well?" (*The New Yorker,* January 23, 1971). And challenging critics who proclaim film primarily a visual medium, Kael asks why film makers buy novels and plays instead of paintings and symphonies. Although of course Kael *can* analyze visual technique when it suits her, as in the *Kane* book, or in her review of *Last Tango*. It is the only movie she's seen that achieves the "effects of expressionism without the use of distortion;" the colors are the "pink of flesh drained of blood, corpse pink." Or in demolishing *Barry Lyndon:* "the film's color fades ominously to a colder tone. This ice pack, coming at the end of the first half, warns us that in the second half there will be none of the gusto we haven't had anyway." (*The New Yorker,* December 29, 1975)

Precise visual description is used by Gilliatt to such an extent that she has been criticized for a nearly "by rote" scene-by-scene listing. This blow-by-blow approach seems—and even looks, for the blocking on the page is such—like small scenarios, or shooting scripts. Gilliatt enthusiasts of course see this rendering as particularly fitting for a critic of film, while for others there is too little interpretation to qualify for criticism. For instance, of Altman's *Three Women,* here describing Shelley Duvall: "She smokes outside the patients' shower curtains; she drinks; she has an alarming, sozzled friend named Edgar . . . who looks like a laid-off cowboy; she drives a snazzy mustard-yellow car that is knowingly nearly matched to one of her dresses" (*The New Yorker*, April 18, 1977). Or on "directions" for an exterior shot, here Warren Beatty in *Heaven Can Wait:* "During a training bout on a bicycle, he has a terrible collision—unseen, thank goodness—in a tunnel with two competitive truck drivers. Enter dry ice. In his sweatsuit, he is now at what is called a 'way station' en route to Heaven or oblivion." (*The New Yorker*, July 10, 1978)

If in her shared *New Yorker* years, Kael became more undisciplined (her endings especially have been an awkward, exhausted, drop-off after a long piece), she also developed a style that was more brilliantly free-wheeling. And if Gilliatt's free associations were "uncritical," they were also splendidly descriptive and evocative of the particular film or individual. Kael's polemics and rabble-rousing may have ruffled the feathers of many of her readers, but they also excited people to take sides in a sudden, Kael-declared controversy. Gilliatt's seeming snobbery irritated some readers, but it provided a previously lacking patina of intellectual elegance and "class" to cinema criticism.

In their particular, different ways, each reacted to movies as other women film critics have: by getting caught up in the rich details of film, and by responding nearly one-on-one to the individuals acting in, or making, the movie. Both critics are extraordinarily enthusiastic about others, sometimes contagiously so; an ironic turn on women's "old" masochistic need to feed on others, to lose the self.

Ironically, the intensity of feelings may have served to short-circuit both: Gilliatt to fanatical adoration and Kael, when not gone rabidly sour on some aspect of a film, to obsessively repeating old passions. For Gilliatt, the aura of glamour surrounding some of the more "special" people in film proved irresistible, as did the temptation to describe the *things* that movies, like fiction, concern themselves with. And for Kael her intense caring for the personalities of the cinema, and for its social implications, found a vehicle in her clever style, which is tending of late to outwit itself. Individually, and without benefit of previous codification, each spontaneously made use of a kind of "montage-criticism" that blends actors' roles with their individual selves while seeing composite parts working as a shimmeringly fluctuating—yet unified—whole.

NOTES

1. John Gregory Dunne, "Pauline," *Quintana and Friends* (New York: E.P. Dutton, 1978), pp. 150-57.

2. Telephone interview with Professor Howard Suber, February 9, 1979, New York-Los Angeles.

2

The Europeans:

Bryher, C.A. Lejeune, Lotte Eisner,
Penelope Houston, and Jan Dawson

While women film critics in the United States held regular reviewing spots quite early—in the 1920s, for instance, Evelyn Gerstein was
reviewing for *The Boston Herald*—no American woman critic, with the
exception of the British born and trained Iris Barry, had an aesthetic
statement set forth, or an overview—in print or elsewhere—of a cinematic movement, type, or national variety. Nor did any American writer
publish a long, sustained critical argument. Yet very early European
women film critics successfully worked as practicing journalists and in
some cases editors while writing books of criticism that were breakthrough, became classics, or at the very least were well regarded.

All the European women critics, early and late, to be analyzed
here—C.A. Lejeune, Lotte Eisner, Bryher, Penelope Houston, Jan
Dawson—are adept at characterizing a director's style, even, in some
cases, of being the first in their country to see that film could be looked
at in that manner. They are all clever at discovering the emotional, at-
mospheric, and historical elements that go into making a national cinema, and most see things from a sociological angle; class structure is a
particularly sharp wedge. We can suggest that this may be because
Europe—being much smaller than the continental United States while
containing so many different cultures and classes—provides ready-made
raw material for such an analysis.

But this does not explain the European women critics' extraordinary, prescient awareness of the importance of the director which later
came to be known as the auteur theory in both the United States and
abroad. Simply stated, auteur theory holds that a film should be looked
at as the creation of one single author, that the true "author" of the film
is its director, and that all of the films created by a director support his
vision. *Village Voice* film critic and Columbia University professor An-

drew Sarris is generally credited with the explanation for and promulgation of the auteur theory in the United States. The two-part American directors study in *Film Culture* 27 and 28 that later became *American Film Directors* sets out the major parameters of Sarris's thinking. It is the working premise for *The American Cinema*, a compilation and categorization of those American directors from 1929–68 who qualify for the title of auteur.

Film historians trace the auteur theory back to the writings of French "New Wave" directors—Truffaut, Godard, Chabrol, among others—in the French film journal, *Cahiers du Cinéma*. Here, during the 1950s, the auteur theory had its beginnings and in the words of British film critic Penelope Houston, the French hoped in some ways to bridge the gap between novel and film. (Yet if women had more input into the auteur theory than has been realized, as I hope to show, this sheds an odd light on feminist criticisms of the auteur theory: that it is phallocentric because it was first defined by men and concentrated only on male directors).

C.A. Lejeune, one of the first women to regularly write about film for the British newspapers the *Manchester Guardian* and the *Observer*, writes in her book *Cinema* on Griffith, Disney, Lubitsch, von Stroheim, René Clair, F.W. Murnau, and others. These directors are assessed against psychological, humanistic, and visual standards. Most important, there is the unquestioned assumption that all films made by a certain director should be looked at in just that fashion, under an auteur umbrella. In 1931, when *Cinema* was published, this is one of the first such groupings of films by directors.

Furthermore, there are the critical areas in which European women critics have not merely predated but completely outstripped their American counterparts, male and female. European women critics and reviewers more perfectly defined the thematic characteristics of various national cinemas of other countries before American critics did. Early British critic Bryher discusses the Soviet cinema in her 1929 book *Film Problems of Soviet Russia*, and Penelope Houston's 1963 *The Contemporary Cinema* treats different national cinemas quite successfully. She discusses the "neo-realistic" or documentary technique of the Italian film, pinpoints the way in which the Soviet character is revealed in its cinema, and has enough insight and distance on the characteristics of her own British cinema to spot the awareness of class structure in British film as well as the "literary" quality of so much cinematic material.

Cinematic style is the other critical arena in which European women writers have broken ground. Not only the individual style of a director, but the style of a national cinema is analyzed by Houston, Lejeune, and—most deeply and referentially—by German-born critic Lotte Eisner. In her 1952 book *The Haunted Screen*, Eisner, by way of explaining the "expressionist" technique of German film makers Murnau, Lang, Pabst, and others, cites brilliantly apt references to history, literature, and art. She sees that the German character is the origin of expressionism, an "extreme form of subjectivism." A visual analysis of cinematic style is supported by an understanding of the national type, a style characterized by "mysticism and magic, the dark forces to which Germans have always been willing to commit themselves."

Yet another European woman critic to see film nationally and sociologically as well as auteuristically was a British novelist and critic, Bryher, a coeditor of *Close Up*, the first periodical to exclusively treat the motion picture as an art form. Based in Switzerland, with an international readership, it was published from 1927–33. Bryher's monopseudonym came about because she did not want to capitalize on the name of her financier father, who controlled many British publications, and who in fact backed *Close Up*. Her real name was Winifred Ellerman; she renamed herself after one of the Scilly Isles. Bryher was married for a time, if in name only, to the film critic and film maker Kenneth Macpherson, her coeditor at *Close Up* and its founder.[1]

Eisenstein, G.W. Pabst, and Gertrude Stein were among those who wrote for *Close Up;* recurrent topics were various directors, technical innovations, and the problems of film censorship. Bryher's reviews and articles for *Close Up* treated mainly educational films, Soviet films, and protests about censorship. "A Certificate of Approval" complains that the English customs office seized a film about Icelandic seals that Bryher was carrying (Vol. 6, 1929). In another piece she writes of a Soviet film, *The General Line*, which may be the "finest educational film ever made," and shows a desolate Soviet village undergoing the sudden intervention of progress, for example, the introduction of anesthesia and birth control, both a shock to those who are used to being treated "as slaves" (Vol. 7, 1930).

Bryher's book *Film Problems of Soviet Russia* is a firsthand account of her visit to the Soviet Union to see the state of the Soviet film. (It got very good reviews in both the *Manchester Guardian* and the journal *Cinema.*) Predating even Lejeune, who had a much wider readership, she writes on individual directors such as Eisenstein, Pudovkin, and Kuleshof. Bryher dubs Kuleshof's film *Expiation* a masterpiece. She devotes a chapter each to the Soviet studio system (the Wufku), the state school of cinematography at Moscow, educational films, and what she calls the "sociological" film. Bryher is unabashedly leftist in the book, although she admits that art has "little to do with politics, but a great deal to do with truth." And sociological truth and utopian possibilities are what delight her. A film, *The Peasant Women of Riazan*, is the "most moral film I have ever seen," since it openly presents not just the "entire core of village life" but a more open sexuality. (She has prefaced all this by saying that childbearing should be left entirely up to the women who very well may be unmarried.) Bryher does not follow through to the next stage in seeing that film might be an instrument for social change; rather, she is simply pleased at its representation. But the sociocultural connection—however tentative—is startling enough for this early period.

C.A. [Caroline] Lejeune was the first woman to start writing about film on a regular basis, first for the *Manchester Guardian* for six years beginning in 1922, then moving on to the *Observer* in 1928. (Iris Barry ran a close second, starting her reviewing career for *The Spectator* in 1923.) The beginning of Lejeune's interest in the cinema is catalogued in her autobiographical book *Thank You For Having Me* (1964), where Lejeune lightheartedly explains her vocational calling. In her last term at college, realizing she was "no true scholar" with "no aptitude for teaching," Lejeune says she knew that her one "small talent" was for writing, but not fiction. After seeing Douglas Fairbanks one afternoon in *The Mark of Zorro,* her "goal in life suddenly dawned." For "I had to be something, and preferably something which would combine writing with the entertainment world. I was not enchanted by the cinema as I had always been enchanted by the theatre, but I enjoyed it. Why shouldn't I turn this enjoyment into profit, and earn my living by reviewing films?" Lejeune says at that time, in the years just after World War I, that this was a rather strange idea for a woman, especially because except for the "women's page" the press in 1921 was exclusively male, and the profession of film criticism had not yet come into being.

In fact throughout her critical career Lejeune had many comments on the requirements for criticism and a personal "philosophy" of criticism and reviewing. An essay titled "'Eyes and No Eyes': What to Look for in Films" is a tongue-in-cheek, clever account of Lejeune's ideas about reviewing. She says that criticism can be formulaic, for "most of us in Fleet Street could sit down and write the same film review in the style of six different papers without turning a hair." Without devaluing the trade, Lejeune declares that most can learn to be a good critic "by using eyes and ears properly." She gives hints to the beginning critic about how to list director's names, producers, and companies (*For Filmgoers Only,* 1934).

In a more confessional vein in *Thank You For Having Me,* Lejeune admits that a critic can have difficulty with certain films because of personal prejudice. She herself had a bit of trouble with *Some Like It Hot* (1959) because she has an antipathy to transvestism, going on to observe that "I believe that any honorable critic, if pressed, would admit to some such idiosyncrasy. It is a weakness which must be recognized, fought and conquered; an exercise which is possible, but far from easy. It is one of the reasons why criticism can never become an exact science: so long as it is practiced not by automatons but by human beings as you and me."

Nor does she claim to be a pioneer of film criticism. Lejeune admits in *Thank You For Having Me* that there were 26 prospective film journalists before her when she approached the editor of the *Manchester Guardian*. (It must be noted here that Lejeune said she had "family connections" at both the *Manchester Guardian* and the *Observer*.) But there is no doubt that she was an extraordinarily devoted critic, reviewing and writing articles for other publications, occasionally writing for television and broadcasting as well. Lejeune, who was born in 1897, was married and had a son. She died in England in 1973.

Much of Lejeune's film criticism stands up today as particularly foresightful. In a 1932 article in *Sight and Sound*, "Films in Education," Lejeune spots the to-be classic 1932 film by Leontine Sagan *Maedchen in Uniform:* it is a "study of the effects of rigidity and repression in a girls' boarding school, sincerely and beautifully handled, with acting of the first order." And an extraordinary column for the January 16, 1926 *Manchester Guardian* is entitled simply "The Women"; it complains that film makers have misinterpreted what might interest women: "When she wants to see horses he gives her children, when she longs for dogs he smothers her with babies. . . . For adventure, domesticity; for the gun, a Paris gown; for the boarhound, a Pekinese."

This might lead us to think that Lejeune is working toward a less "sexist" aesthetic, in that women didn't really crave the stereotypical subject matter afforded them in the 1920s. But that would be anachronistic, for she has a few standard notions herself. She feels that women are bored by slapstick and disgusted by scenes of cruelty and deformity. It is important that producers understand this, according to Lejeune, since the vast majority of cinema goers are women and always will be. They will always be happy to leave the home, where their work is, to go to a film. While the sociological realities of women home makers may have changed, Lejeune has certainly hit on the vicarious nature of cinema going for women. Just so, woman is "fiercely, desperately personal, and the kinema the most personal of all the arts" (Lejeune here retains the original Greek spelling of cinema). In a loose theoretical statement she decides that the star system, with its emphasis on personality, fills a need for women which the other arts cannot. And this familiarity makes her a great critic, according to Lejeune, for she loves what she criticizes, and that with the "keenest intuition." However, the familiar complaint about the lack of "great art" from women stumps her, (not even fantasizing, as Virginia Woolf does in *A Room of One's Own*, a sororial equivalent—albeit a frustrated one—for Shakespeare). At least women have borne men, she reasons, who have produced great art. And the privacy and passivity of the film-going experience, even the darkness, the "sleepy music," the "chance to relax unseen" are all "woman's pleasures."

Lejeune's concepts about the personal, intimate nature of the cinema have freed her to analyze the "star personality," especially in her major book *Cinema* where so many of the trends of her work come together. Like future European women critics Simone de Beauvoir and Claude-Edmonde Magny, Lejeune is not afraid to attach special significance to the ouevre of a particular actor or actress. While by now—after the impact of a Pauline Kael—we are not unused to seeing actors considered from a sociological angle, or as they affect an audience, no serious American critic before Kael dared to mix in biographical information about an actor with an interpretation of his or her work, or to analyze film *according to* all the works in which a star appeared. An auteur theory of acting, as it were. One might conjecture that this is because Americans have had a built-in prejudice against a movie magazine-ish approach to "serious" criticism.

But in Europe, rigid stratifications of "highbow" and "lowbrow" have seemed less required. It may be that Europeans have a more self-confident and less self-consciously puritanical attitude toward culture. In any case, Lejeune includes wonderfully insightful chapters on Mary Pickford, Douglas Fairbanks, and, as we might expect, Chaplin. The impact of Pickford, who played ingenue parts even as an adult, is analyzed: we see Pickford "through our own experiences blurred with time. What we like to think we were—what we like to believe we felt and dreamed—the way we imagine we used to see life—all this is implicit in the Pickford films. Children see in Mary themselves plus an enchanting remoteness towards maturity; adults love in her themselves minus sophistication and age." And Lejeune uses information about Pickford's "real" life to elucidate—in an early kind of psychobiography—her success on the screen. Pickford "grew from a sage, business-like, determined child to a sage, business-like, determined woman, who could exploit unerringly, and had the courage to exploit, all the emotional frailties in human nature that make for a player's popularity—and success." Moreover, admiration for Pickford in the film community seems tied in with reverence for the parts she played.

Even more surprising is Lejeune's piece on Douglas Fairbanks. While admitting right off that he "cannot act, cannot move dramatically, and cannot speak his lines without extravagance," Lejeune decides that Fairbanks is still one of the few figures of the American cinema who stands for "something imaginative and fine." But she doesn't limit herself to analyzing his impact on the audience, or his sociological effect;

Lejeune boldly and openly declares that, although Fairbanks has never formally been a director of one of his films, he carefully chose other actors, directors, and technicians who would reflect his "spirit," his "stamp." Even so, he was probably unconscious of his own flair for beauty in the cinema. The "bubbling streak" of visual poetry exists within extraordinary popular success in films which, intellectually, may only say that it is "a fine thing to be alive" or that exhibit a breezy kind of American sportsmanship.

It's not as startling to note Lejeune's good essay on Chaplin in *Cinema*, for by 1931 a number of pieces had been written about him as both director and actor; yet in addition to some nice descriptions of Chaplin's commedia dell' arte method, Lejeune attempts to look at the *whole* of his work; we talk about Chaplin's comedies "as though they formed one indivisible mass of work"; we discuss in one breath Chaplin the director and Charlie the clown, and assess Charlot's every manifestation as a single created whole. And we are right in our instinct, for only the sum of Chaplin is the real Chaplin since "a balance of qualities" carries the "essential meaning." (André Bazin's observation in his essay on Chaplin that "Charlie is a mythical figure who rises above every adventure" was published in 1948.)

Other motifs that Lejeune finds are prophetic too, some of trends not codified even today. In *Cinema*, Lejeune writes on the "experimental film" (what we today might call the avant-garde film), on the "News-Theatre" (probably the documentary, for the cinema is the "natural journalism of today") and on the new position of the "camera-man" after films have "gone talkie." It has taken years, Lejeune asserts, for an audience accustomed to seeing the inportance of the star to recognize the director; she doubts "whether one man in a hundred would be prepared to stretch that recognition to the technical staff." Yet, after mentioning a number of outstanding cameramen she says it is "interesting to notice the affinity, in every country, between the best of the directors and the best of the cameramen." In her book, Lejeune even devises the categories of "Films of Travel" and "Films of the Soil," the latter being the one that didn't hold up so well. And like most European women film critics, Lejeune seems to naturally gravitate toward observations about national cinemas and styles; for example, there is a chapter on the Soviet cinema.

Most of *Cinema*, however, is devoted to various directors. There are pioneer chapters on D.W. Griffith, Ernst Lubitsch, Erich von Stroheim, René Clair, and Walt Disney. Lejeune believes that Griffith gave directors a new freedom of expression, "entirely independent of the spoken word." He taught them the way to "use their cameras for comment and emphasis, how to cut for suspense, how to combine major and minor story values in one broad strand of continuity." Griffith discovered new narrative devices, and also "how to multiply the movements of a small number of figures into the movement of a multitude, how to set the whole of an action pulsating by the use of contrasted pause." It is interesting here to compare Lejeune's comments with Eisenstein's in "Dickens, Griffith, and the Film Today." Eisenstein's 1944 essay is more technologically sophisticated, yet a number of the same main points are emphasized: the importance of narrative and the significance of the rhythms and pauses of editing for some.

Yet if Griffith's contributions, according to Lejeune, are "technical, not personal," Lubitsch is designated the "first emotional director of the European cinema" who, when he started work in the United States, also managed to catch "the pace and quality of American life in his cameras, and very deftly, very gently, turned it to ridicule." It is of course much to Lejeune's credit that she spots the significance of the cartoons of Walt Disney, although they are "just" cartoons. Disney managed to "cut away the whole tradition of the static and the theatrical" and work "with the belief that sound should liberate movement, not cramp it, that dancing should grow out of music, and rhythm out of dancing." Not only, of course, are they "imaginative, witty, and satisfying," but (and here Lejeune gives a sociological rationale for art similar to that proposed by other European women critics, particularly Eisner) Disney's cartoons are important because they, like Soviet propagandist films, are completely of their age. And "any art that is strong and valid is the definite social expression of a civilization."

While there is no place where Lejeune codifies her directorial standards, "Retrospect," the introduction to *Cinema*, provides some insight into what such a code might be. Using Hitchcock as a negative example, while still asserting her regard for his craftsmanship and his "shrewd common-sense, unhampered by tradition," his ability to "observe and chronicle," Lejeune denies that he is a great director. He doesn't have "warm humanity" or "psychological insight." And a review in the January 12, 1941 *Observer* begins: "What Shaw is to literature, Chaplin is to the cinema. The great thing about the Chaplin films is that they are all Chaplin. . . . I am all for dictatorship in film making. A single man whose yea shall be yea and whose nay, nay." Lejeune says she wants one man "whose signature on the film represents final and incomparable authority. I am well aware that such a system would quickly put half the current directors out of business." But that would be all right with Lejeune, for, significantly, a "director who does not take full responsibility for his pictures has no business to be in the business at all." The key concepts of the auteur theory—even the phrase "signature on the film"—are evident here, in 1941.

In her book *Cinema*, Lejeune is apt to make quick characterizations of various national cinemas, some of which still apply today. After describing the "tangibility" of every physical detail that contributes to the creation of such a strong atmosphere in the Swedish film, namely the "pressure of stones," the "touch of the old wood," the light becoming a "physical experience," she decides that with Scandinavians, moreso than with others, "we get a vivid sense of inborn life in every stick and stone," for "the craftsman merely gives utterance to a mute energy, develops a power already lying dormant." Style is taken here quite fully into the realm of meaning. Decades before Bergman appeared on the scene, Lejeune has decided that the "old personification of the elements has never quite left the Scandinavian mind, and wind, wood, water is still alive; light and darkness are still elementals." Examples are the work of Danish film maker Carl Dreyer, and the Scandinavians Mauritz Stiller and Victor Sjostrom. The work of Greta Garbo is mentioned here too.

Lejeune observes in a chapter on "France and Feyder" that the French cinema could be characterized as being brilliant but sporadic: "tentative, theoretical, groping, insecure." Each individual film is a "mass of bright patches on a dull substance." National character and cinematic style reflect each other then as Lejeune makes a nice, if fanciful, reverse connection between the Soviet development of montage and the impulse to strip down celluloid to its basic state—the worker, farms, tractors, and so on—that are the "plain," component parts of the Soviet film. And while in the United States a kind of mythic interpretation of the cinematic western did not occur for at least another 20 years, Lejeune can presciently observe that in westerns "what really matters . . . is not that a man and woman should eventually come together, but that a new world should be opened or a community freed."

Lejeune is precisely descriptive on certain aspects of montage. In her chapter on D.W. Griffith, she explains that the director was really the first to use what she calls "constructive cutting." After disparaging the fact that in 1931 montage is thought of as a "new thing in the cinema," Lejeune notes that the early director made innovative uses of the close-up, of crowds, and especially of movement. And with his application of montage, he could "whip up image to a tornado, wring the last drop of pathos, and set an audience tingling in a perfect ecstasy of suspense." Lejeune cleverly summarizes the difference between Griffith's use of montage and the Soviet technique: the American director tends to use "the group instead of the single frame" and for more sentimental ends.

Lejeune's reviews are good working examples of her theory. In discussing a German film, *Warning Shadows,* in the *Manchester Guardian* (November 24, 1924), Lejeune touches on style as representative of national character. The film comes "as all the films of mental exploration have come, from Germany, and fitly epitomizes the production of a country which has always borrowed from shadows its fullest power, painting with darkness where the Frenchman would paint with light, lengthening its shadows, deepening its shadows, endowing its shadows with a life and character all their own." And the importance of the director is underscored in her review of *The Magnificent Ambersons* ("The Magnificient Welles," 1943). Welles has style, if one cares only about who "marries whom and who did what, this is not the work for you." For "Mr. Welles is one of the few directors who scrawls his signature across every scene. He accepts no ukases nor conventions; he sets his camera roaming to find the new approach to the old situation; he will shoot an actor from the roof, the basement or the coal-scuttle if the fancy takes him; the sound track gives him a free world to range in." It is for Welles as if 50 years of the cinema did not exist before; the cinema is a "fresh page for him to cover with his bold, characteristic handwriting." Too, Welles can be "arrogant and superb," even "almost patriarchal" (cf. the spoken credit title at the film's end "I wrote the story and directed it. My name is Orson Welles.") Similarly, 18 years before *The Third Man* in 1949, Lejeune catches on to the directorial skills and style of Carol Reed; he is a "brilliant all-round craftsman" who "enjoys making films as films, and isn't choosy about his subjects."

The shorter reviews occasionally miss. Although Lejeune generally is good at characterizing American films, she is puzzled by the impact of *Gone With the Wind.* To the question "What is the secret of *GWTW*'s success?" Lejeune comes up with no good answer. It does not have the "emotional appeal" of *Mrs. Miniver,* the "magic" of *Snow White* or *Bambi,* the "fertile invention" of *Citizen Kane,* or the "elemental force" of *The Grapes of Wrath.* It is "not even the longest film ever made." It is only a "blessed distraction" in wartime (the film was released in 1939). Even so, "catastrophe without contemplation is no tragedy, and even amongst all those dead and dying, our emotions are seldom over-tired." This time, Lejeune's ability to analyze the sociological impact of the American film fails her.

And while Lejeune praises Olivier's 1944 film *Henry V,* which has "springtime ardour," her praise is a bit trite; we are given the chance "to come to Shakespeare fresh, to discover his magic anew, and I for one am grateful for it;" it is "a beauty," "delightful," and so forth. Usually, however, Lejeune is more psychologically astute. Hitchcock, who seeks to preserve security in his own home, has a cathartic talent for telling a story "in which the security of middle-class life is savaged by fearful crime" (review of *Shadow of a Doubt,* 1943). Or she observes that—in a discussion of war films—"when a man's mood is disturbed, he is quicker to catch the mood of others" (*The Gentle Sex,* 1943).[2]

Possibly the European woman critic who brings the most complex intellectual set of references to bear on the cinema is Lotte Eisner, a critic and film journalist who has lived most of her life in France and who, as of this writing, still resides in Neuilly-Sur-Seine, France. Eisner, born in Berlin in 1896, studied archaeology. She wrote for a number of German newspapers, including the Berlin *Film-Kurier,* before leaving Germany before the Nazi take-over ("Heads will roll," one Nazi editorial warned about Eisner's film writing). As a film curator, she worked with archivist Henri Langlois in setting up the Cinémathèque Française, the prototype for the idea of a cinémathèque (a place where films are screened and studied, sometimes read about), an idea that has been internationally imitated. She is the subject of two documentaries. In one, *Lotte Eisner in Germany* by S. Mark Horowitz (1982), she comments on her own surprising resurgence of interest in the "New German Cinema" (the films of Werner Herzog, Wim Wenders, Rainer Fassbinder, et al.) for she declares that she thought she would never care for German film again. Even so, she wonderfully describes the geographical sweep of Herzog, the typically German urban movement of Wenders' characters.

Perhaps more important than all of this, Eisner is the author of a number of highly readable yet densely referential books on various film makers and national cinemas. She has written books devoted to F.W. Murnau (director of the classic films *Nosferatu,* 1922; *The Last Laugh,* 1924; and *Sunrise,* 1927) to Fritz Lang (director of the famous *Metropolis* in 1926 and *M* in 1931), and she is the author of the seminal *The Haunted Screen: Expressionism in the German Cinema and the Influence of Max Reinhardt* (published in France in 1952), a book that takes into account much of the German character and history in explaining the cultural movement of expressionism, what she terms an "extreme form of subjectivism." Specifically discussed are the German film makers Murnau, Pabst, Lang, and Lubitsch (although the latter is placed outside the mainstream of German expressionism). After some vivid descriptions of the style and surface of these film makers' works, Eisner, with many historical references, can declare that the best German directors have limited themselves to tragic films, possibly because while others, she asserts, may have a taste for life, the Germans have a taste for death. Moreover, the "wierd pleasure the Germans take in evoking horror can perhaps be ascribed to the excessive and very Germanic desire to submit to discipline, together with a certain proneness to sadism." Expressionism, Eisner decides, attracts the Germans because it is an outgrowth of "mysticism and magic, the dark forces to which Germans have always been willing to commit themselves." As a Jew who has lived in Germany, escaping to France on the eve of World War II, she describes Germanic faults with relish. The book contains many photographs and examples from literature, painting, and history to support her assertions.

It is interesting in this context to compare the treatments that Lejeune and Eisner give to Murnau's *The Last Laugh.* Lejeune informs us in her book *Cinema* that while *The Last Laugh* may be Murnau's least sensational film, it is surely his most significant (as opposed presumably to the more well-known *Nosferatu).* It is important for us to remember that in 1931 posterity is not helping Lejeune here although her decision may certainly have been borne out. She decides that *"The Last Laugh* was the first film with definite camera continuity." Lejeune is enthusiastic, though not eulogistic or particularly partisan, about the film. Rather, it is the development and shape of the cinema as an art form that concerns her. Eisner on the other hand explains that *The Last Laugh* could only be a German story, since it centers around the fact that a hotel porter, proud of his livery, must become a lavatory attendant: This could only be a tragedy "in a country where the uniform (as it was at the time the film was made) was more than God." Camera angles are used, Eisner points out in *Murnau,* to make the man look bigger so that images "taken from a low angle emphasize his cheeks and his pompous importance, in the manner of Soviet films. Pictures taken from high up make the poor wretch in the washroom seem more and more seedy." Style equals psychology, which often reveals national characteristics. Eisner uses cultural, psychological, and sociological references in the broadest possible sense.

Eisner accepts an auteur theory of the cinema, too.[3] But she actually traces the first "auteur" theory in *The Haunted Screen* to the German notion of the *Autorenfilm,* a movement established around 1913, some 35 years before the more familiar auteur theory. This "idea of a film being judged as the work of the author" is no surprise, Eisner says, coming from a country with as strong a literary bias as Germany; naturally the strength of the German cinema owes much to the notion of the "literary scenario." Of course Eisner's own work supports the importance of the director, in her two books—on Murnau (1953) and Fritz Lang (1977), and in sections of *The Haunted Screen,* particularly those that have been excerpted and widely anthologized, such as "Pabst and the Miracle of Louise Brooks." G.W. Pabst's style in the film *Pandora's Box* (1928) and *Diary of a Lost Girl* (1929) is shown to work at great advantage because of the "remarkable" Louise Brooks who is "endowed with uncommon intelligence," and is "not merely a dazzlingly beautiful woman."

Eisner is especially acute in analyzing style, especially as it derives from social class. She explains the component parts of the creation of the "Lubitsch touch," the style of German director Ernst Lubitsch, which was characterized by elaborate costuming and high frolic. A native of Berlin, Eisner traces Lubitsch's petit bourgeois humor to his identity as a Berliner.[4] Before Hitler, she notes, the residents of this city were a "realistic and even materialistic people, with a keen sense of the ridiculous and a fondness for backchat." Added to this is the impact of various groups throughout the city's history; the French wit of the Huguenots, the intellectual drive and insight of the Jewish bourgeoisie. Then finally the "nonchalant, rather cynical humor of the Jewish lower-middle class," who were engaged in the garment trade, those who also embodied the fatalism that results from being subjected to pogroms and persecutions. This may seem to be making too much of the historical background and the influence of social class, perhaps because Americans, compared to Europeans, aren't accustomed to seeing cultural phenomena over such a long historical perspective, or to considering class stratifications (at least, not openly so).

No film critic or historian, American or European, brings as many and as wide art historical references to bear on film as Eisner. (Vachel Lindsay would seem an obvious exception, but it is simply not so.) She can tidily compare Murnau to Watteau, in citing the "voluptuous pallor of a woman's décolleté, or the nuances of a silk gown in a profusion of darks and lights" (*The Haunted Screen*). Paul Wegener's *The Golem* (1914), with its "alternately terrified and exultant crowd" recalls the "flamboyant outlines and disjointed movement of a painting by El Greco." Sets used in Paul Leni's *Waxworks* (1924) seem to anticipate the creations of Antonio Gaudi, according to Eisner. And in Murnau's *Faust* (1926), the choirboys surrounding Gretchen's pillory are "open-mouthed, innocent, unaware, like the beautiful ambiguous angels in Boticelli." Eisner cites the "the art historian in Murnau" with his ability to organize a set. The entire concept of chiaroscuro, or alteration of light and shade, is the underlying leitmotif of *The Haunted Screen*, since chiaroscuro with its extreme contrasts perfectly represents the emotional intensity of expressionism.

Visual style is a forte of Eisner's, as one might expect from her background as an art historian. The "success of the admirable opening of *The Last Laugh* is entirely due to the handling of the camera . . . Murnau's camera exploits all possible visual resources." He likes, for example, to join "mobile camera effects to the effects of shots through a pane of glass." Best of all is when Eisner's talents as art historian and film critic can merge, as in her piece "The Painter Reveron," a review of a film by Margot Benacerraf in *Sight and Sound* (autumn 1955). Eisner observes that it "is rare that a director succeeds in creating a personal, dramatic rhythm from his material, like Emmer and Gras, and like Alain Resnais in his *Guernica*, where each image was like a cry, and the sudden swooping camera movements interpreted Picasso's apocalyptic vision."

Though Eisner and Lejeune may have been the first European women critics to focus on elements of social class, Penelope Houston also sees film in this way. In fact, a case might be made for the fact that Houston's best writing is on films with a heavy class emphasis. Houston, who started as a freelance reviewer for the *Spectator* and the Sunday *Times*, first published in the spring 1949 issue of *Sight and Sound.* She became an assistant editor of *Sight and Sound* in 1951, and wrote a column, "Scripting," in 1951. Periodic reviews appear as well, and in the mid-1950s Houston started to write central articles, concentrating for the most part on thematic concerns or covering film festivals. In 1956 she became an editor of *Sight and Sound.*

In Houston's book, *The Contemporary Cinema* (1963), there are sociological explications of films such as *Saturday Night and Sunday Morning* (1960) and *A Kind of Loving* (1962), as well as the film from which she takes a chapter's title, *Room at the Top* (1959). She is expert at spotting the class distinctions inherent in the British social system in order to analyze the structure, intent, and atmosphere of films. An existence in a "semi-detached" (a British term for a kind of duplex), a "grey, grimy, and desperately restricted life" are examples of urban squalor that become metaphors for the hero's state of mind. So does even what passes for sport: a "grim jousting in the mud" (*This Sporting Life,* 1963). Houston's fitting and fetching analogy to hero Joe Lampton's adventures in *Room at the Top* is to the hero of Stendahl's *The Red and the Black.* He is the "classic young man from the provinces, the Julien Sorel of an English north-country town."

Room at the Top, in fact, is a paradigm for this kind of film. Its setting is the requisite industrial landscape, the dialogue one of "hard-shelled brusqueness." There is the "occasional piercing moment of self-revelation" as well as the "near ritual beating-up" and the pub scenes. An article in the spring 1959 *Sight and Sound* places *Room at the Top* in the broader context of the "angry young man" genre in the theatre and the novel in both England and America, although Houston is careful to note that while *Room at the Top* may not be a great film, it is "vigorous, compelling and of the moment."

The Contemporary Cinema finds the same "neorealistic" class consciousness in the Italian cinema of post-World War II, particularly in the films of Visconti, Rossellini, and de Sica. And—with a bit of sophistry—Houston decides that even 1960s films like Antonioni's are just one more reworking of realism. Like other European women critics, Houston sees national character revealed in the film; the Soviet film is "puritanical about sex, sentimental about children, irreproachably Victorian in its morality." She explains nicely the economic and cultural forces at work in Hollywood (particulary the effects of the McCarthy witch-hunts and the growth of television), which shaped the "careful" American cinema of the late 1940s and 1950s. And Houston seems to have gravitated more and more toward American films, as her shorter pieces for *Sight and Sound* and other periodicals show. Houston must be given credit, too, for calling attention to the Japanese cinema in *The Contemporary Cinema* (in the United States, critics Donald Richie and Joan Mellen are usually given these kudos) and for citing the subtle and sensitive work of Indian director Satyajit Ray, whom she likens to Renoir in that he "looks, and looks, and looks again."

In *The Contemporary Cinema*, the aesthetic assumption is—not unusually—that the cinema is' essentially a collective art, despite the fact that the importance of the director goes unquestioned. Cameramen and screenwriters may be mentioned, but a work is analyzed according to the director's "touch," or by its narrative content, as when Houston discusses the "fugitive" heroes of Carol Reed. She is especially fine on *The Third Man*. And in her description of *Jules and Jim* in her chapter on the French film and the *nouvelle vague* she states that Truffaut finds the exact cinematic style for his subject matter. A "nostalgia for innocence" is indicated by editing in actual newsreels of World War I. The result is enchanted, "like a man running down a long, sunlit road with a camera in his hand." Auteur premises are to be seen, too, in Houston's shorter work (see, for example, her piece on Hitchcock, "The Figure in the Carpet," *Sight and Sound*, autumn 1963).

While in many of Houston's shorter pieces topicality may take the place of more meaningful "trend-spotting," a good survey is offered in "Hollywood in the Age of Television" (*Sight and Sound*, spring 1957). But the overview is not deepened to a larger significance. Houston is drawn to the American films that seem to yield ready sociology, as is evident in her reviews of *Marty* (*Sight and Sound*, summer 1955), *Giant* (*Sight and Sound*, winter 1956–57), and *Cat on a Hot Tin Roof* (*The Observer*; 1957). Too frequently she summarizes plots and too often writes in clichés: Ernest Borgnine in *Marty* is breaking away from thug parts such as a "chillingly brutal stockade sergeant" to act with "expansiveness" and "warmth of feeling."

Houston is less trite in her *Sight and Sound* column, "Scripting," where she can explain in a January 1950 piece what *All About Eve* and *Sunset Boulevard* are about to her British readership, to wit: "A beautiful young actress is receiving the theatre's highest award; *All About Eve* tells her story. As a stage-struck girl she is befriended by a middle-aged star, dominant," and so forth. There is nothing really "wrong" with Houston's analysis of this film, or of *Sunset Boulevard*, or of *Marty* either, and often she finds felicitous phrases to describe a film's action. As her review of *On the Waterfront* shows, she pinpoints "the cocksure, gum-chewing arrogance" of the hero (Marlon Brando). And, like other women film critics, she is frequently clever in picking out just the right descriptive detail, as he is "aimlessly pulling on her glove while they [Brando and Eva Marie Saint] talk."

A historical, thematic "tracing" like Houston's "Glimpses of the Moon" (*Sight and Sound,* April-June 1953) has fine descriptions of science fiction films of the 1950s and some early prototypes. The article is thorough, obviously well-researched, and "responsible." But we can observe here some of the more mediocre virtues of Houston's critical work—dramatic action, plot, and character are her chief concerns. And she too has the film critic's tic so common to many: the embroidered cross-referencing as one film, director, or actor reminds the writer of another film, another director, and so forth. Perhaps critics of all the arts are subject to this sometimes irritating habit, but the cinema's richness of detail makes it particularly susceptible. It is an interesting comparison to analyze Houston's science fiction piece side-by-side with Susan Sontag's more original "The Imagination of Disaster," which takes the sci-fi film down to its component parts without referring just to earlier sci-fi films (this essay is collected in *Styles of Radical Will,* 1969).

Only an occasional piece of Houston's in *Sight and Sound* attempts a critical statement, like "Leading the Blind" (spring 1959). Here she simply repeats some oft-observed thoughts: that the cinema is the work of "many artists," that the weekly critic does not have the "austere concentration" of the textbook writer who can focus only on the highest art. She puts the "average" life of the critic at about ten years: three to learn, four to practice, and three more to forget. After which one may become "a hack, a cynic, a defeatist." Her standard aesthetic ideas are observable in a column "In Perspective" (*Sight and Sound,* March 1951), in which she asserts that in the cinema, "all is change," for it has no traditions or solid body of academic criticism "to act as a balancing factor." Houston concludes, using a simplistic aesthetic, that this is why a national cinema may rise and decline and a technical innovation be explored and then outdated. It is all "part of the cinema's constant and necessary preoccupation with the immediate present."

She does much better, as we see later in the article, in discussing the literary quality of British films (and in seeing that most of the best postwar films have come from literature). For like the Italian postwar neorealistic cinema and the demonic German cinema of the 1920s, British films take their character from the social or cultural forces pressing upon the cinema. This stimulates energy and realism, and is just one more reason why, in a circular way, "in the cinema, everything is contemporary." The same *good* observations, of course, are found in the *The Contemporary Cinema.*

Many women critics have written for *Sight and Sound,* including Iris Barry, Bryher, Pauline Kael, and even mystery writer Dorothy Sayers. One present-day writer who has appeared quite consistently in the pages of that journal is Jan Dawson, a freelance writer and translator who is presently preparing a critical history of the New German Cinema and who has published a monograph on German film maker Wim Wenders. Her reviews and articles have appeared in journals such as *Film Comment,* the British Film Institute's *Monthly Film Bulletin,* and *Cinema Papers.* She also produced the English dialogue script of *The Story of Adele H* for Truffaut. Like Houston, although without the editorial tie-in to *Sight and Sound,* Dawson has written many reviews and articles for *Sight and Sound.* She seems to "get" many American films for review but she also writes on the films of the "New German" film makers like Werner Herzog. Her very positive review of *The Mystery of Kasper Hauser* (or) *Every Man for Himself and God Against All* appears in the autumn 1974 *Sight and Sound.* She interviews Wim Wenders in another *Sight and Sound* as part of an article on Patricia Highsmith, the author of the novel that was the basis for Wender's 1978 film *The American Friend,* and the 1976 monograph on Wenders includes his critical writings and interviews by and with Wenders.

Her reviewing style—somewhat more complicated than Houston's—can be observed in her review of *One Flew Over the Cuckoo's Nest* (1975). It is appreciative of director Milos Forman's ability to work in various genres (one of his first American films, *Taking Off,* was a treatment of life in suburban New York done with the flavor of cinéma verité). Yet Dawson finds much to criticize in *One Flew Over the Cuckoo's Nest.* There is a strong critical consciousness here, declaring that the "realistic representation of electroshock treatment has no place in an ebullient comedy of hospital manners." Moreover, Jack Nicholson's "stellar" performance is "out of tune with the hesitant naturalism for which the other inmates strive." Styles clash overmuch for Dawson. There is too much disparity between "the realism of sets, symptoms and surgery," and the "far-fetched and highly structured artifices of the plot." Dawson's writing is generally insightful and not clichéd, and one feels that, as her November 30, 1973 review of *Paper Moon* for *The New Statesman* shows, there is a historical and critical depth here that would bode well for a major work. Dawson begins her review with a comparison to a nineteenth-century French dramatist, Labiche, who wrote light comedies: "It would be a tragic waste, after the visionary promise of *The Last Picture Show,* if Peter Bogdanovich were to emerge merely as the Labiche of the contemporary cinema." And Dawson sees that the problem with the film is that "Bogdanovich has planted his fragile fable in an American Midwest still squirming from the Depression (not an era many of us can contemplate with unqualified nostalgia)." In the United

States, some of the more thoughtful critics, Penelope Gilliatt, John Simon, Paul D. Zimmerman of *Newsweek*, Jay Cocks of *Time*, and Vincent Canby of the *New York Times*, found fault with the film, while so many others praised it. It is in some respects fitting that a "foreigner" was able to spot some off-base cultural assumptions about the American social scene.

All the European women critics discussed here, both early and late, pick up on the definitive characteristics of a national cinema, and view films from both a sociological and class-oriented perspective. Lotte Eisner may be the most precise in defining visual style, but Lejeune— especially when one considers the "early" status of her work—is surprisingly on target describing the work of individual directors as well as the qualities of various national cinemas. She is of course not an "intellectual" like Lotte Eisner, so her observations about national character as revealed cinematically do not have the weight of historical analysis behind them, as Eisner's do. Lejeune's are more the conclusions of an intelligent observer, as are Houston's. In Houston's case, however, the uniqueness of originality is missing, and the conclusions are a bit more superficial. Of all the critics with class awareness discussed here, Bryher is the only one using such analysis for a political purpose, as vague as her focus may now seem. (Harry Potamkin may have seen things from the Marxist point of view, but the intent to change society via film is not there).

Each of the Europeans either accept or posit the importance of the director (the auteur theory). And, as we have seen, two of them, Lejeune and Bryher, may in some sense be seen to have "founded" this approach to film, if in a more matter of fact and less self-conscious fashion than later theoreticians who claim the theory. No grand announcements or pronouncements, just a quiet putting to work. One may make a case, too, for Lejeune's early literary analogizing to montage. Houston, Lejeune, and Eisner were, and Houston still is, functioning reviewers as well as critics. In this sense they may be compared in the United States only to critic Molly Haskell, for up until the 1970s no woman reviewer-critic in the United States simultaneously held a reviewing post and wrote books of criticism (Kael's and Crist's books are, after all, collections). On this pioneer and "feminist" issue, then, as well as on the grounds of being the first in developing at least some semblance of an auteur theory, the European women critics were groundbreakers. And in the analysis of a national style of cinema, they have not yet been surpassed.

NOTES

1. For a detailed discussion of Bryher's attachment to poet H.D. and their involvement with film and *Close Up*, see *H.D.*, a biography by Janice S. Robinson (Boston:

Houghton Mifflin, 1982).

2. Reviews of *The Magnificent Ambersons, Gone With The Wind, Henry V,* and *Shadow of a Doubt* are all collected in *Chestnuts in Her Lap,* a selection of Lejeune's reviews for the *Observer* from 1935–46.

3. Though she is critical of *Cahiers du Cinéma*—the major spokespiece for the auteur theory—for being "too political." See an interview with Eisner in *Filmmakers' Newsletter* (February 1974).

4. Continuing in her ironic vein, she ultimately points out that when Lubitsch arrived in the United States he decided to "rid himself of a certain 'Central European' vulgarity," including the "frequently oafish effects in his middle-class comedies." *The Haunted Screen,* p. 79.

3

The Feminists:

Molly Haskell, Marjorie Rosen,
Joan Mellen, and Laura Mulvey

It seems inevitable that two areas of great intellectual excitement in the last half of the twentieth century—film study and the woman's movement—should eventually have crossed paths. It was just as likely, in retrospect, that the amalgam would result in the rapid development and application of a feminist film theory. For film had not yet been conceived when the first wave of feminism broke in the nineteenth century, and was just a youngster during the early part of the twentieth century when the suffragette movement, the second major feminist campaign, gained strength. In retrospect, it seems most likely that the formal study of women and the analysis of film would coalesce after the political movements of the 1960s, and some films of that decade, raised questions about "out" groups. That the "new sensibility" about women was not reflected in the films of that era spurred the development of a feminist film theory in what most cultural analysts think is the third great flowering of feminism in Western society. In addition, the very nature of image, or iconography, is visual. And it is to an awareness of the visual elements in film that some feel the recent critical schools—semiotics (the science of signs) and structuralism (analysis according to relationships)—owe their origins. With female images comprising at least 51 percent of the composition of movie frames, there is automatic material for the semiotic-structural approach. Yet even within the parameters of a feminist theoretical overview we can observe the same traits of other women film critics: a tendency to personalize, to see the work of an actor or actress as oeuvre, and—more than anything else—to stress the strong reciprocal influence of a "star" on its culture.

Naturally we may expect recent criticism to reflect a raised consciousness—uplifted, admittedly, in varying proportions—in critics and audiences. Yet feminist film criticism, especially when applied to narrative content and character analysis, can too frequently be no more than the grafting of the "new sensibility"onto film: this or that character is or was not "liberated" enough. This anachronistically gray area is one in which many feminist film critics have lost their footing. There have been attempts to justify, in some twisted way, Katharine Hepburn's suicide over a man in the 1933 film *Christopher Strong;* since both director Dorothy Arzner and Hepburn are automatic feminist favorites this was an unfortunate natural. In the film Hepburn, as Lady Diana, commits suicide while flying her own plane on discovering that she is pregnant by her married lover. Yet a forced feminist rereading such as Molly Haskell's in her 1973 book *From Reverence to Rape* declares that Diana's decision to pull off her gas mask is prompted by the stress of trying to reconcile her aviation career with the demands of a family. Career, a lover, and a family are too much for any one woman, Haskell implies (a theme picked up in much of her other writing), but the important point here is the deliberate omission of certain narrative elements.

And there are forced arguments that apply a patina of feminism to earlier films, like critic and screenwriter Marjorie Rosen's in her discussion of D.W. Griffith and his heroines in her book *Popcorn Venus* (1973). Rosen treats the particularly independent nature of the lead role in *Judith of Bethulia* (1913), which starred Blanche Sweet: "More likely than not, Griffith as well as the audience was oblivious to his radically profeminist approach; and none of his filmed characters after Judith was allowed her independence or power." If only D.W. (and his viewers) had known! Such a superimposition is valid only in a quaint history of ideas approach; at a later date it might be of some slight interest to see the attitudes of 1973 imposed on an earlier set of data. More important, one becomes reduced, along with the author, to the pinpointing of certain "accepted" notions: here's a female image with the right approach, there's one without. *Popcorn Venus* uses the decades of the twentieth century as chapter divisions, with a fast socio-pop background beginning each chapter. And then there is the complusive pointing out, categorizing, and judging of what meets or fails to meet the standards of the women's liberation movement.

Molly Haskell's more stylistically and referentially sophisticated *From Reverence to Rape*, coincidentally, has the same organizational pattern, with its thorough sense of historical comprehensiveness. The problem, however, with a format based on a decade division, is that there are bound to be overlaps and overgeneralizations. Yet Haskell's analytical approach is not, as is Rosen's, a simple-minded *Life* magazine-ish survey of the American cultural scene. Instead, the method she uses to arrive at the same conclusion, that there is a lack of suitable film roles for women and that the roles that do exist are degrading, is at least partially a psychoanalytic one. The "time line" merely provides a framework.

One of the most ingenuous—if obvious—aspects of feminist film criticism has been the strong identification of individual critics with the roles and stars they see on the screen. The merge of actress and role seems to be a specialty of women film critics, but the teenager-like "crush" (with no homoerotic overtones) is peculiar to both Haskell and Rosen. In their respective introductions to *From Reverence to Rape* and *Popcorn Venus* they report their earliest cinematic idol to be Margaret O'Brien. For Haskell, it was "not for any role in particular but for the twin privileges she claimed as movie star and tomboy. She was a few years older than I, with long, sleek pigtails that were the model for my own short, stubbornly vagrant ones." Later, taking the safe side in the double standard, she "chose" Audrey Hepburn and Grace Kelly who had "artistocratic cool" rather than the "sexual profligacy and vulnerability" of Marilyn Monroe, Elizabeth Taylor, and Jennifer Jones. Rosen says—curiously focusing on the same detail—"Margaret was my idol, and if my braids weren't as long or as neat or as beautiful, well, it was my mother's fault, not mine." Later, *Jules and Jim* "couldn't have been anybody but me and my two dearest male friends at college in Ann Arbor." All feminist criticism, whether working with positive (and sometimes negative) role models as these critics do or in deconstructing mainstream film as the feminist-structuralists do, posits the direct influence of film on the lives of women, far and away more than some lighthearted observations about the male undershirt industry being in trouble when Clark Gable did not wear one in *It Happened One Night.*

Neither Haskell nor Rosen knew of each other's work-in-progress until a great deal of the research and writing had been finished on each book.[1] Their common theme must have come as a shock to each, since until 1973, there had been no book-length feminist treatment of women and film and not even one by a woman that attempted to survey the entire American cinematic scene. Haskell had been working as a freelance film critic in New York since the late 1960s and had written articles for film journals as prestigious as *Film Comment* and *Film Heritage;*—mainly complimentary auteur pieces on Godard, Hitchcock, and Murnau. While working at the French Film Office she met and married Andrew Sarris. She soon began to review films regularly for the *Village Voice* and has been an influential member of the New York film community ever since, writing for middlebrow magazines such as *Vogue, Viva,* and *New York,* as well.

Haskell brings to bear two critical tools that Rosen does not. Neither of these beliefs is new, yet both are deeply ingrained in the American intellectual tradition, which explains why Haskell's work has been so firmly embraced by the literary community. Underpinning *From Rev-*

erence to Rape and many of her magazines articles is a positive belief in a Freudian theory of sexual repression. The other intellectual "axe" is the generally accepted conception of the suffering artist. Yet, despite the aura of intellect that is added to her self-proclaimed feminism, a curious conservatism is the result. And if the profeminist arguments in the book succeed, it may have to do simply with the numbers of films cited as supporting examples. At the time, too, many were "discoveries"—lost or little-known films. This has been a valuable contribution of *From Reverence to Rape;* as important is the recognition of the "women's film" as genre.

Yet in an article in the June 1973 issue of *Mademoiselle,* "Can a Woman Have a Good Marriage, Children, a Satisfying Career, a Social Life, and a Super Sex Life All at the Same Time?" Haskell dismisses Wilhelm Reich and Norman O. Brown, who endorse the theory of the simultaneous release of sexual and creative energy. She goes on to assert "But the evidence to the contrary is overwhelming. Almost every human being who has excelled . . . has done so by developing some faculties at the expense of others." Haskell also claims that "the wound of sexual unfulfillment spurs the bow of artistic achievement," with a nod in the direction of critic Edmund Wilson's use of the "wound" image for the suffering artist. Wilson employs the classic myth of Philocetes's "suppurating" (offensively dripping) wound to declare that the artist— like Philocetes—may be necessary to cure a sick society, although he himself must bear the burden alone.[2]

Translated into feminist film criticism, these neo-Freudian and romantic notions result in Haskell's strongly psychoanalytic interpretation of certain actresses and directors, for instance: "And yet to the extent that he is an artist, the director is driven to create by some maladjustment, however minor: by the wound, the stutter, the irritation, the limp that keeps him out of step with the world's drummer. Directors with the most lavish film fantasies, Ophuls, Sternberg, Lubitsch, Cukor, for example were often short or unprepossessing men who were able, luckily for us, to live through and for magnificent women." So that for an artist-director, "the wound, the social and sexual malformation, becomes both cause and effect. Women will be made to reflect his puritanism, his obsessions, his hostility, just as the men created by a feminist novelist will be made to reflect her disenchantment and bitterness" (from *From Reverence to Rape*). The "neurosis" of each ten-year period changes as we see it transferred from director to actress, and magically transformed into a symbol—albeit embodied in a beautiful actress—of society's illness. Here the example is D.W. Griffith, but Haskell mentions the films of John Ford and John Huston as well. It is no wonder then that she doesn't recommend a complete expression of sexuality for directors, since the impetus for creation would be destroyed. And while she sees the maimed director and the victimized actress as responding to the needs of a society repressing women, a deeper reading of *From Reverence to Rape* and Haskell's essays and reviews reveals her pseudo-psychoanalytic bent to be a cover for personal arch-conservatism.

Other pieces are more overt. An early article by Haskell in the April 13, 1972 *Village Voice* claims that the "screen's sexual liberation of women has been, in many ways, [woman's] psychological undoing. Just as the repressive Production Code drove directors to find metaphors for lovemaking, so women who express themselves sexually are apt to be reticent in other ways." That sexual activity results in shyness (particularly for women) just as repression results in metaphors of lovemaking is a logical connection that doesn't make it. Of course it argues against sexual liberation for women; it also points to Haskell's push-pull theory of sexual energy in general. Later in the same article she declares "There may be a Reichian superwoman of whom sexual liberation is not accompanied by a shrinkage of other muscles, but I've never met one. (There's Germaine Greer, but I've only seen her on television. And besides, she's Australian.)" And although she might later disclaim this "early" statement, it's still worth noting: "To me, women's liberation has always been more powerful as an idea than a movement, although I readily concede it is the movement which keeps the idea alive and burning in the bosom of a recalcitrant public. But liberationists are guilty of the god-like desire to remake womankind in their own image."

Much of this flip quality is toned down in *From Reverence to Rape*, as one might expect, even though the book was published in 1973, only a year after the *Voice* article. Yet the same syllogisms underlie her thinking. A series of rhetorical questions in the introduction sets out the parameters of Haskell's conjectures. There is a determinism here so fixed as to make any Freudian feel hemmed in, as she asks "whether it is possible to disentangle the neurotic and imprisoning aspects of love from its positive, and liberating ones. Whether a woman's propensity for 'total' love is basic or conditional. Whether insecurity and dependency are crucial or incidental factors in that love, and whether such liberating devices as the pill, in removing those factors, remove the conditions of love. Whether a woman's professional advancement and diversification will leave less room, and less need, for love. Which is to ask whether, in removing the props and crutches of love, we will remove love altogether." Haskell clearly thinks so, from the structure of the oppositions she sets up. This would be all right, except that it is love Haskell is sorry to see go. Nor does "liberation" seem to aid even those women's roles she sees as not demeaning. Which thereby explains the depressing conclusion to her book: that there simply have been no decent cinematic roles for women.

In a review of *Looking for Mr. Goodbar* (1977), where the role

Diane Keaton plays is at least a major one, Haskell connects liberation with violence as she equates predatory singles bars with "the demons that the rhetoric of liberation has released" (*New York,* October 31, 1977). A review of director Martha Coolidge's 1976 autobiographical documentary about rape, *Not a Pretty Picture,* is sourly titled "Rape Rakes It In" (*Village Voice,* April 26, 1976). Haskell complains that the film "takes to its extreme the woman's school of documentary in which film becomes a form of self-therapy." In all fairness, however, Haskell is usually quite uncompromising on the subject of rape (it's more the "sixties self-expression" that seems to get on her nerves). In fact, rape often seems to be a red flag to a bull for Haskell—an easily recognizable feminist tag.

But even Haskell's protest piece about the film *Snuff,* about which it was rumored that an actress was actually murdered during the act of sexual intercourse, blames the violence implicit in some pornography on liberation. In "The Night Porno Films Turned Me Off" (*New York,* March 29, 1976), Haskell complains that in "a society in which clothes (real and figurative), words, and conventions are a lie, and civilization is an overlay of hypocrisy, the only 'authentic' human being is the one who exposes his ego in all its greed and rapacity." She is satirizing the behavior of those who "epitomize the pseudologic of the liberated sixties." And she ends her piece by declaring that she hopes to "close the book on porn" by urging critics to "return to an Aristotelian sense of moral responsibility."

If Haskell's approach is darkly, demonically psychoanalytic, Marjorie Rosen's work seems too frequently simple-mindedly sociological, or else tritely, patly feminist. Rosen, currently a film and TV scriptwriter, had published very little film criticism before the publication of the 1973 *Popcorn Venus.* She has written for few journals devoted exclusively to film except *Jump Cut* and *American Film.* Rosen explains her lack of a "pure" film aesthetic by calling herself a popular historian. Besides, she declares, economic realities have forced her to mix journalism and criticism for some of her magazine pieces such as those for *Ladies Home Journal.*[3] Rosen, since the mid-1970s, has periodically reviewed films for *Ms.* magazine. One may argue that her reviews for *Ms.* contain some responsible feminist thought, but her attitudes are always very much in line with the *Ms.* stance, with certain topics and film makers getting automatic boos and raves; rape, and Martha Coolidge's *Not A Pretty Picture,* come immediately to mind. Rosen admiringly underscores Coolidge's on-screen testimonial that, because she was raped as a teenager, as an adult Coolidge still can't have a good relationship with a man.

Rosen may not lay heavy claims to being a "serious" critic. Still, an article in a magazine like *American Film,* clearly no heavyweight critical or theoretical forum, is full of the same easy generalizations as *Popcorn Venus* and—suspiciously enough in the case of *Grease*—is written "on the set." Even the partisan pushiness of Pauline Kael can't be matched by such promotional fluff as Rosen offers here (and for a movie like *Grease*, which even the casual observer can see endorses the double standard for 1950s women). Even temporary nostalgic lustre was transparent. Rosen praises "the look of the production . . . bright and buoyant colors rather than the pinks, silvers, and charcoal grays [which were] certainly not as dowdy as they actually were in the fifties" (*American Film*, February 1978). Never again can Rosen complain, as she does in *Popcorn Venus*, that Hollywood whitewashes reality, since a camp verisimilitude is about all *Grease* has to offer.

Like critic Andrew Sarris, Rosen frequently falls back on personal reminiscence (as does Haskell, but to a lesser degree), not just in this piece but all through *Popcorn Venus*, thereby sliding over a deeper critical probe. Similarly, a superficial pop sociology combined with the kinds of generalizations found in *Psychology Today* (a magazine that she quotes as source material in other articles) inform Rosen's analysis of even so perfect a feminist subject as Marilyn Monroe:

> Almost entirely she played the delicious dumb blond with both head and heart as soft as a cotton ball. . . . Although Marilyn was learning her craft, the schism between her ambitions to play such roles as Grushenka in *The Brothers Karamazov*, and Twentieth's—to have her ring-up more dollars through tired rehashes like *How to Be Very Very Popular*—engendered her walkout. . . . Marilyn has, in death, been immortalized by those who see her as a symbol of total masculine and industrial exploitation. This is true. And false. . . . Marilyn's inability to throw herself into work in times of trouble suggests that despite herself, she had deep in her heart bought the traditional notions of feminine values. Love, or at least desirability, restored her. For when she was in trouble, unsure of herself, she would return to the comfort of the image she obsessively wanted to wipe out.

Clearly Rosen is on "safe" grounds here, since we all know enough about Monroe to fill in some blanks. It *is* a nice surprise that Rosen prefers to take a mixed rather than a unilaterally sympathetic view of Monroe. But this unfortunately reads like a gossip monger column in a bad movie magazine (the "intimate" use of Monroe's first name throughout is just one tip-off; condescension, naturally, should be no part of any feminist credo). Rosen's analysis comes off poorly in comparison to Haskell's, although many points are similar, particularly the tie-ins to the culture at large. But a much more literate and literary style elevates Haskell's prose (as in the paraphrase of Mary Queen of Scots's final speech before her execution that in her end is her beginning, which concludes the following paragraph):

> Our feelings about Marilyn Monroe have been so colored by her death and not simply, as the uncharitable would have us think, because she is no longer an irritation or a threat, but because her suicide, as suicides do, casts a retrospective light on her life. Her *"ending" gives her a beginning* and middle, turns her into a work of art without a meaning.
>
> Women, particularly, have become contrite over their previous hostility to Monroe, canonizing her as a martyr to male chauvinism, which in most ways she was. But at the same time, women couldn't identify with her and didn't support her. . . . The times being what they were, if she hadn't existed we would have had to invent her, and we did, in a way. She was the fifties' fiction, the lie that a woman has no sexual needs, that she is there to cater to, or enhance, a man's needs. She was the living embodiment of half of one of the more grotesque and familiar pseudo-couples—the old man and the "showgirl," immortalized in *Esquire* and *Playboy* magazines. [emphasis added]

(*From Reverence to Rape*)

Haskell's subsequent discussion of films like *The Seven Year Itch, Niagara, Some Like It Hot* also make use of a similar critical analysis that combines both woman and role. (In discussing *Some Like It Hot*, for example, Haskell concludes "Marilyn, the little girl playing in her mamma's falsies, the sex symbol of America, is right there where the dream turns into a cartoon and back into a dream again").

Rosen does better with Mae West, acknowledging that West is independent and in control of her destiny. But she sees her as a counterrevolutionary force in West's "masochistic" presentation of herself as a sex object. An interesting idea, but Rosen supports this reading only by the most simplistic psychoanalytic observations: "This camp quality was Mae's greatest asset—and perhaps her liability, too. As a parody, she didn't take herself seriously; therefore, few others did. Men could laugh good-naturedly at her audacity; it wasn't threatening because Mae was *not* a potential conquest—she was one of the boys, and her banter borrowed from an elevated locker-room sass. For women, she had neither the beauty nor the youth to pose a moral threat or example, and furthermore she deliberately made certain that no dialogue or action would disenchant her female audiences." Rosen here ignores the historical facts, the censorship difficulties that effectively ended West's career, although *Popcorn Venus* usually relies on sociological facts. Moreover, while it is careless for Rosen to imply that only youth and beauty can provide a moral threat, it is downright reckless on feminist grounds for her to say, in a discussion of the exaggerated costumes West wore, "the irony is that while all females suffer and starve to some extent for fashion, Mae's was an unnecessarily masochistic kind of extreme vanity which she overworked as her trademark." Vanity and self-torture in moderation only, please! (Quotes above from *Popcorn Venus*.)

A much more rigorous feminism is to be found in the work of Joan Mellen, a professor of film at Temple University. Mellen writes from a radical leftist and occasionally Marxist perspective, particularly in discussing the treatment and representation of women in the cinema. Her viewpoint is so consistent, in fact, that she has been accused, with some justification, of perverting the interpretation of certain films and roles. At least the discipline prevents the overly facile identification of critic with star that is found in the work of journalistic critics.

Mellen's tendency to maintain a possibly overconsistent point of view may come from the fact that she is both a Marxist and a trained academic; even so her extremely prolific output of books and articles has provided a wider critical berth than that afforded most academic critics. Since the late 1960s, her articles on various directors, films, and adaptations of literary works have appeared in *Film Comment, Film Heritage, Cinéaste, Literature/Film Quarterly,* and others. She has published a collection of essays on women and film, *Women and Their Sexuality in the New Film* (1973), and on men and the cinema, *Big Bad Wolves: Masculinity in American Film* (1978). Mellen has also written books on various films and directors, including *Filmguide to The Battle of Algiers* (1973) and *The World of Luis Buñuel* (1978). Some would credit her, along with critic Donald Richie, with turning U.S. critical and popular attention to the Japanese film in her books *The Waves at Genji's Door: Japan Through Its Cinema* (1976) and *Voices from the Japanese Cinema* (1975), although it's clear that England's Penelope Houston "got there" first in *The Contemporary Cinema.* Superimposing her Western feminist standards on Japanese films in her exposure of the obviously patriarchal setup of Japanese society has irritated some specialists who see her generalizations as both deliberately distorted and ignorantly crude at once. Mellen's critical breakthrough came with her feminist work, most particularly in essays collected in *Women and Their Sexuality in the New Film.* As a Marxist, true, but also as a woman, her ready sympathies lie with the "out" group, the exploited.

Mellen is brilliant when the inherent class structure of a certain film lends itself to her schemata, as her discussion of Bertolucci's *Last Tango in Paris* (1973), demonstrates.[4] If the film, paradoxically, "is not *about* politics, it is more political than either *The Spider's Stratagem* or

Bertolucci's *The Conformist* (1970) because it explores how people are affected by the dominant values of the time, seeking in sexual release a means of escape both from the social past and from the personal history of characters." Mellen can be as psychoanalytic as Haskell, although analysis is yet another prop for her political vision: "Brando-Paul experiences feelings as inseparable from rage and violence because this association occurs when deep needs are repressed from earliest years. And he can risk their expression solely in an insular, artificial environment isolated from bourgeois reality because the violence outside is not merely the concomitant surfacing need, but cold unfeeling brutalization and murder." Class structure and a historical overview are the poles around which Mellen's psychological insights and sexual observations converge. The same holds true for her discussion of the beautiful and vulnerable lesbian Anna, played by Dominique Sanda, in *The Conformist.* (Quotes above from *Women and Their Sexuality in the New Film.*) Being an outsider, a non-Fascist, and beyond mainstream sexuality all seem connected; ultimate victimization is apparently fitting, as the final murder of Anna indicates.

Yet her frequent preference for Eastern values over Western "decadent" values (read capitalism equals perversity), combined with a more enlightened view of censorship and pornography than Haskell's, comes through in her treatment of Oshima's 1976 film *In the Realm of the Senses* (1976), as a *New York Times* article published July 31, 1977, shows:

> In its uniquely Japanese approach to love, *In the Realm of the Senses* utterly transcends Western pornography, even though we are witness to the sexual act. The idyll of Sada and Kichizo, devoid of brutality, offers delight for both the man and the woman. Unlike pornography, and following the tradition of erotic art by Japanese wood-block printmakers like Utamoro and Hokusai, the love scenes focus on the sexual ecstasy of the woman. . . . Sada pleases Kichizo by her enthusiasm and we learn that she was so successful as a prostitute because she was happy and enjoyed sex so much— another particularly Japanese point of view. . . . People continually happen in upon the lovers, but such intrusions are treated with humor, not prurience, just as the lovemaking is presented beyond the claims of puritanical morality.

The conclusion of the film, which bothered so many critics (who have clearly forgotten or would rather not remember Elizabethan expressions of the bliss of dying in the act of love just as they suppressed that the film was based on historical fact) with its murder and dismemberment of her lover by the prostitute, is nicely explained away by Mellen: "But Kichizo's death is freely chosen as a gift to his lover, that she may 'be happy strangling me.' Dying, he sees everything 'in red,' reminded of his birth in this vision where death is as natural a phenomenon as sex. As in Western thought (cf. de Rougemont), love and death are finally facets of the same experience."

It is true, however, that Mellen's often politically inspired insights may seem periodically dogmatic, especially when she tries to tie in too many elements that are not necessarily connected. This is the case in the introductory essay in *Women and Their Sexuality in the New Film,* which gives an overview to the essays in the volume. In a piece entitled "Bourgeois Woman: A Disturbance in Mirrors," Mellen reasons "that there are fewer films about strong and independent women today than there were in the 1940's is attributable in the United States to a capitalism in moral decline," but this is not fully explained. And she occasionally falls into the same trap that Rosen and Haskell do, by judging women's roles according to personal standards of feminism or liberation, deciding in the same chapter: "Thus in the 'new' films, women are no longer coy, but they lack all personal integration. They are not presented as finally fulfilled by the husbands they catch, or shy as they whisper in hubby's ear the news of the blessed event. But they have no purpose or fulfillment; in place of acting coquettish they are shrill and unseemly." Again, these subjective observations do not necessarily comprise a critical stance or make a case without some theoretical underpinning.

Yet feminism, when wedded to a coherent critical position, provides a sharp wedge into some films. Then Mellen's critical judgments are of a more permanent nature, and avoid the topical quality of her chapter "Lesbianism in the Movies," which too frequently becomes a mere cataloguing. Instead, the sociopolitical approach combined with a deep knowledge of woman's historical place can enable Mellen to see a director like Bergman in a larger context. The essay, in her book, is "Bergman and Women": "It is largely through woman, the creature tied to her flesh, that Bergman pursues the theme of man as a humiliated victim of a cosmic joke whose dictates can never be transcended nor its purpose fully grasped or accepted. The debasing sexuality of his women is fated as long as there is a human race. They are powerless, inherently unable to organize their lives differently, as with the young girl in *The Virgin Spring.*" One might paraphrase Mellen to say that if man, or mankind, is in an embarrassingly animalistic state, as Yeats observed, the real onus is carried by womankind, less readily spiritual even than man.

Mellen was the first major American critic to see Bergman's treatment of women in a mainly negative light. Most critics were euphorically bamboozled by the fact that women, after so many years of inattention, were getting any kind of focus at all. (One exception is Swedish critic Barbro Backberger who censured Bergman in her 1962 book on him.) Rosen is particularly culpable in this regard; while Pauline Kael disliked much of Bergman from an early date it is on grounds of his "self-indulgence" and his compulsive self-analysis. Haskell sees that Bergman's handling of women reflects his own unfortunate double standard; still he has "provided us with an array of women characters as rich and complex as those of any novelist" (*From Reverence to Rape*). It remains for Mellen to put Bergman's entire opus in a broader historical and deeper metaphysical context. For Bergman, she observes, women are limited by their physical (or menstrual) selves, isolated—as man is too, to be sure—except when lust takes over. To reject such love-lust, of course, only results in loneliness; but the real Catch-22 for women is that "lust in women for Bergman is usually directed toward a man who cares little for them, who in fact mixes his passion wih contempt." Finally (and here Mellen speaks of the 1972 *Cries and Whispers*) the "hatred of women for men is unabated. . . . It is as irrevocable and inevitable as life, as the blood red fades to the 'normal,' pointing to woman's special shame."

Of course it's clear that Mellen does not advocate any of these attitudes; in fact her prose, where she speaks of "special shame," only barely falls short of using quotes for irony or contempt. Rather, there is "something both inauthentic and suspect in an artist who delights in enclosing his women characters in a cycle of pain based on physiology at a time they can move beyond what they have been. In fact, Bergman has made victims and martyrs of his women at precisely the moment when they are rapidly rendering obsolete his vision of their 'nature'" (quotes above from *Women and Their Sexuality in the New Film*).

Both Mellen and Haskell analyze style and structure as a means of getting at a film's meaning, while Rosen's work is singularly lacking in this area. In treating *Last Tango in Paris* in the same essay discussed above, Mellen can find metaphorical structure and the theme of the film by analyzing the editing: "He sits on the floor and cries in desperation, an effective cut from his life with Jeanne to that with Rose, indicating through the editing that the two relationships are essentially similar, and ultimately evoke similar emotions." As Mellen shows, the rhythm of editing points up congruencies in much the same way that structural symmetry has been traditionally seen as indicating parallelisms in literature; the perfectly worked out symmetry of language and structure in *Pride and Prejudice*, for just one.

Mellen can comment successfully on the emotional coloration of style as well: "The frequent tilts [of the camera] also convey the motion of one life merging into another." And in a *blend* of style and structure that many see as the imagistic "poetry" of film, Mellen picks up on the metaphorical possibilities of a single shot. She speaks of the heroine in Kurosawa's *No Regrets for Our Youth* (1946): "A shot of the torn blossoms floating desolately in the basin of water where she has thrown them expresses the irreparable rupture in the life she has known."[5] Mellen's training in literature may make her more sensitive to nuances of what used to be known as a new critical, or textual, analysis. Yet Haskell can also provide a primitive kind of structural analysis, as her treatment of the very same scene in *Last Tango* shows, "Schneider's journey under Brando's instruction into her own entrails (her sodomizing by Brando-Paul) is a terrifying one, but if she emerges she will be in such possession of herself that she won't have to hold on for dear life anymore" (*From Reverence to Rape*). A metaphysic surrounding the image is hinted at, if not fully explored or explained.

Mellen is thorough in speaking of tone. Red, she notes, is the symbol of sexuality in *Cries and Whispers*, a point made by many critics. But she is more original in her treatment of the opening sequence of *Last Tango:* "A woman brushes false teeth in the toilet as Jeanne enters a cafe to make a phone call. In a flood of yellow light Paul passes her, the use of yellow in this film recalling Eisenstein's brilliant essay on Color and Meaning in *The Film Sense.*" But she does not fully explain or underscore the connotations of such coloration, although we know from his essay that Eisenstein uses examples from T.S. Eliot's poetry and Rembrandt's self-portrait at age 55 to demonstrate that yellow (as he is careful to differentiate from gold) connotes both a sense of sin and the tragic passing of time.[6] Of course it's not necessary to elucidate every reference one makes, but it is a familiar writer's ploy to toss off a crucial reference without seeing it through. In the case of Mellen on *Last Tango* it's a significant omission, since the topic is style.

One critic who does fully integrate aesthetics into her feminist credo is Laura Mulvey, a British writer and film maker only now gaining wide recognition in the United States. Mulvey is associated with the semiological approach to film that, in combination with her particular brand of Marxist-Freudianism, sees film as a weapon with which to do battle against a phallocentric, capitalistic society. Mulvey is married to Peter Wollen, author of *Signs and Meaning in the Cinema* (1972), a work that uses the semiotic approach to film. She considers her films, *Penthesilea* (1974) and *Riddles of the Sphinx* (1978) to be her most important work, although she has said that her political commitment has prompted her to put her ideas into print. Paradoxically, her intended subversive semiotics has led Mulvey to a concern with style, aesthetics, and a kind of surface or textual analysis; what she might consider reactionary methods of criticism.

Mulvey uses semiotics to decode a film, whereby the "real" message of movie may be reached, she believes. For the sign (what is shown, or the image) is often at odds with the connotation (what is "really" meant), notwithstanding semiological debates about which element, signifier or signified, is the most important. Mulvey determines that the surface, especially in the case of late-1940s and 1950s films, opposes the narrative line, thereby functioning in a radical or revolutionary fashion. Admittedly, as with all semiologists, it sometimes seems, the precise method of interpretation remains a mystery. But since Mulvey arrives at some acceptable feminist conclusions about sexuality and repression the results aren't too hard to swallow.

In her discussion of Douglas Sirk's *All That Heaven Allows*, a 1956 film in which a couple from different social classes and age brackets (the man is untraditionally younger than the woman) plan to marry despite bourgeois disapproval, Mulvey points out that as unusually "progressive" as the narrative line is, the "true" message is embodied "as the shutters are opened in the morning, [and] the cold, hard light of repression is driven off the screen by the warm light of hope and satisfaction."[7] Mulvey can link colors with emotional states, an analytical technique that Mellen takes a stab at and Rosen and Haskell don't even try. (See Haskell's treatment of the same film in *From Reverence to Rape* where she merely notes that Sirk "is not stylistically timid" or her admittedly superficial comments in an interview in the "Women and Film," winter 1975–76 issue of *Film Heritage* where she gushes that *All That Heaven Allows* is "fantastic" especially in the heroine's recognition of her selfish children: "It's so refreshing to have these awful children.") Mulvey sensitively observes that the film world of the hero "is divided between the cold, hard light (blues and yellows) of loneliness, repression, and oppression and the warmer, softer light (red/orange) of hope, emotional freedom and sexual satisfaction."

"Visual Pleasure and Narrative Cinema" is a more austerely theoretical article, and one that is unfortunately more typical of Mulvey's too frequently awkward and jargon-ridden style. As stiffly written as it is, this piece contains Mulvey's clearest statement of intent for feminist film criticism: "Unchallenged, mainstream film coded the erotic into the language of the dominant patriarchal order. It is said that analyzing pleasure, or beauty, destroys it. That is the intention of this article." For if woman in her "to-be-looked-at-ness"—Mulvey's construction—is necessarily passive, the attraction for the male (since according to Mulvey most films to date reflect either the male director's or male character's point of view) will become either "fetishistic scopophiliac" or "voyeuristic-sadistic." Ultimately, she reasons, even when an actress succumbs to the male figure and thereby identifies herself with him, she becomes a threat, since it is her mere physical being—her lack of a penis—that implies the possibility of castration and therefore "unpleasure." The traditional male solution to the anxiety of castration fears, according to Mulvey, has been to make the female figure a fetish. (*Screen* 16, no. 3, autumn 1975).

One may balk at this loose Freudianism and certainly at the prose style (viz. "Ultimately, the meaning of woman is sexual difference; the absence of entrance to the symbolic order and the law of the Father"). But Mulvey's work has provided an important centrifugal force for other more traditionally respected critical elements: Marxism, Freudianism, and psychoanalysis. More important, British and American feminists have been able to find the connections in Mulvey's work—albeit tenuous, awkward, and sometimes forced—between films, phallocentrism, and patriarchal social order. Mulvey argues, in a stance that is widely respected in academic film circles, that woman's oppression and male dominance are central to the basic structures of mainstream cinema. And the concept of male film makers as voyeuristic in their use of female body parts has filtered down to popular feminist criticism (see especially Veronica Geng's review-essay on *Personal Best* in the March 18, 1982 *New York Review of Books;* Geng defends director Robert Towne by claiming that he uses body parts in a nonvoyeuristic, nonsexist, and pleasantly unself-conscious way). Other British women film critics who have worked in this theoretical mode are Claire Johnston and Pam Cook. Both use the work of Freudian psychoanalyst Jacques Lacan in combination with semiology and the auteur theory—and myriad other influences, some Marxist, some linguistic—to formulate a feminist film theory more systematic and formidable than the more spontaneous, descriptive, and loosely "sociological" approach of their American counterparts.[8]

Prior to this, as we have seen, objections to certain films and feminist rereadings of others, have been both helped and hindered because they have had no particular critical school to defend or promote, at least not in the United States. Molly Haskell has said that this critical freedom has been what has attracted women critics to film; with nothing to either lose or defend, a greater analytical and intuitive freedom is allowed.[9] One of those freedoms—as can be observed in the work of Rosen and Haskell on Marilyn Monroe—has been to simply blend an individual woman with the role she plays. Joan Mellen uses a similar approach, employing psychobiography much as Haskell does. Mellen's *Marilyn Monroe* (1973), the first American book-length treatment to use only this method, observes that the "split between early feelings and consciousness underlay her prolonged crisis of identity as Norma Jean versus Marilyn or sex symbol versus serious actress. She could not commit herself to either of these roles for long." This is more rigorous than Rosen's handling of the same topic—Monroe's "inability to throw herself into work in times of trouble."

In their treatment of Mae West too we can see a similar approach at work. In the essay "The Mae West Nobody Knows," Joan Mellen asserts that West always maintains control over the two most important aspects of her film life. First, she always has a hard-to-hold-down or "masculine" job, such as a lion tamer or outlaw—the latter a comic reworking of Belle Starr, the woman rustler. Second, she is always turning off, or on, the men in her life. Moreover, Mellen asserts, West does not use men as mere sex objects; the implication is that she is far beyond 1970s women in films where a heroine frequently uses macho tactics in reverse. Thus West is autonomous, sexually active but not promiscuous: "She transcends the cultural meaning of sexual availability in women because she separates it from servility and servitude." (*Women and Their Sexuality in the New Film*). In this we see the same assumption that Rosen has made about West.

C.A. Lejeune posited this much earlier about Chaplin, Pickford, and others, saying that they were in control of the roles they were performing in. For Haskell, so complete was West's androgyny "that one hardly knows into which sex she belongs, and by any sexual-ideological standards of film criticism, she is an anomaly—too masculine to be a female impersonator, too gay in her tastes to be a woman." And so she fits nicely into a feminist credo: "If anything, Mae West shows that certain qualities thought to be incompatible—'male' concupiescence and aggressiveness and 'female' romanticism and monogamy— can coexist" (*From Reverence to Rape*).

The composite view underlies her responses to male stars as well. A *Village Voice* article "The Great Hollywood Con: Machismo Doesn't Live Here Anymore," which assesses the new nurturing male, decides that Spencer Tracy, James Stewart, and John Garfield were actually more honestly sensitive and emotional than the highly touted Kris Kristofferson, Jon Voight, and Alan Bates figures in vogue in the late-1970s. Haskell's real favorite, however, is John Wayne, and it is a preference traceable to an earlier adulatory article for the *Ladies Home Journal,* "Wayne, Westerns and Women," in which she praises his stubborn and roughhewn qualities, identifying Wayne with her father, and querying if this is why she wants to be a "little girl" when she sees him (July 1976).

Haskell's personalizations, which are endearing and enlightening in the introduction to *From Reverence to Rape,* can brilliantly demonstrate the culturally paradigmatic possibilities of individual response. The back and forth leap from screen to self to culture that is a trait of women film critics can descend into coyness, however, as the Wayne worship above shows. Too, an April 1978 piece in *Film Comment* unfortunately titled "You Gerard, Me Jane" admires Gerard Depardieu for his "primitivism": "Depardieu gives every sign of being the genuine article, sexism and brutishness intact . . . [we] . . . immediately con-

nected. He was all there, playful, grinning; there were no barriers between us. He grinned at me occasionally between takes, and I grinned
back. Possibly I blushed." (Haskell is visiting the set of Bertrand Blier's
Get Out Your Handkerchiefs.)

Haskell, probably more than any other woman critic, is most commonly associated with feminism in the popular consciousness. Yet at
this writing she reviews most regularly for *Vogue* and *Playgirl,* hardly
feminist strongholds, although it is clear that pieces can appear at her
will in *Ms.* the *Voice,* and occasionally as segments on National Public
Radio. Rosen reviews for *Ms.* periodically, communally and cyclically
sharing reviewing spots with other *Ms.* writers. She has said that the
current state of American movies makes them unworthy of intellectual
examination; therefore she will not write another book about films because while thinking about movies in 1971 was like thinking about yourself that's just no longer true.[10] Joan Mellen's work, while known to film
aficionados and scholars, does not have a wide readership in that she
does not review for a mainstream periodical. Laura Mulvey of course
does not write about the cinema regularly, and at least half her written
work appears only in British magazines; her main thrust is her own film
making.

In England, the "radical" journal *Screen* continues to publish the
feminist criticism of film critics Pam Cook and Claire Johnston. But it's
not readily available to American readers. The devoting of special issues
to feminist film criticism by various U.S. film journals, like the "Women
and Film" issues of *The Velvet Light Trap* and *Film Heritage,* seems to
have had its day. The important periodical *Women and Film,* founded in
Berkeley in 1972 and designed to criticize not only Hollywood's misuse
of women but to discredit the male-oriented auteur theory, ceased publication in 1975. Its former editors and writers, Julia Lesage, Patricia
Erens, Beverle Houston, Marsha Kinder, and others, now write for other
film publications.

Three anthologies have appeared in the late seventies that treat
women in film. *Women and the Cinema,* an anthology put together by
Karyn Kay and Gerald Peary, collects 45 essays on the general topic of
women and film, most of which have been previously published. The
editors don't even try for a theoretical overview, after admitting that
contradictions "leap out from one article to another." *Sexual Strata-
gems,* edited by Patricia Erens in 1979, contains a number of valuable
essays by Lesage, Kinder, Claire Johnston, and Lucy Fischer among
others, but most of the pieces in this volume were previously published
in various periodicals. E. Ann Kaplan's edited work *Women in Film Noir*
was published in 1978. It contains significant essays on the classic, but
"progressive" mainstream film, such as *Gilda* and *Mildred Pierce,* which
can be reanalyzed by using iconography and structuralism to undermine

a patriarchal system.

Only *Camera Obscura*, a journal begun in the early 1970s in California and still published there, is exclusively devoted to feminist film criticism. It is a collectively edited periodical publishing articles that are theoretical in nature and often quite difficult to follow. Even so, it refuses to be pinned down to any one critical position, or to say whether or not women view films differently than men do. A multiplicity of voices on the topic should be required, according to one of its editors.[11] Platforms, outlets, organs and voices seem few and far between in the early-1980s, which is in dramatic contrast to the near-militant rage about film's use and abuse of women that characterized the early- to mid-1970s. Feminist film criticism may now seem to be an institution, but it has few practitioners.

NOTES

1. Telephone interviews with Rosen and Haskell, August and October 1979, New York City.

2. Edmund Wilson, *The Wound and the Bow: Seven Studies in Literature* (New York: Oxford University Press, 1947).

3. Telephone interview with Rosen, August 1979, New York City.

4. Is this one reason why she names Bertolucci, along with Visconti and Costa-Gavras, as involved with "the most interesting and challenging work being done in the film today?" "Fascism in the Contemporary Film," *Film Quarterly* 24, no. 4 (summer 1971):2-19.

5. Joan Mellen, "A Reassessment of Gilo Pontecorvo's *BURN!*" *Cinema* 7, no. 3 (winter 1972-73): pp. 121-24.

6. Sergei Eisenstein, "Color and Meaning," Trans. Jay Leyda, in *The Film Sense* (New York: Harcourt, Brace and World, 1942), pp. 121-24.

7. "Notes on Sirk & Melodrama," *Movie*, no. 25 (winter 1977-78), pp. 53-56.

8. Johnston has edited *Notes on Women's Cinema* (London: Society for Education in Film and Television, 1973); *The Work of Dorothy Arzner: Towards a Feminist Cinema* (London: BFI, 1975); and, with Pam Cook, *"The Place of Women in the Films of Raoul Walsh,"* in *Raoul Walsh*, Phil Hardy, ed. (Edinburgh Film Festival, 1974). *Notes on Women's Cinema* was the first publication in English of a feminist and materialist approach.

9. Haskell interview. On this topic, see E. Ann Kaplan, "Interview with British Cine-Feminists," in *Women and the Cinema: A Critical Anthology*, Karyn Kay and Gerald Peary, eds. (New York: E.P. Dutton, 1977), pp. 393-406.

10. Rosen interview.

11. Interview with editor of *Camera Obscura*, who preferred to remain unidentified; March 1982.

4

The Reviewers:

Judith Crist, Dilys Powell,
Renata Adler, and Janet Maslin

For many people, especially those who are not film aficionados, film criticism means just one thing: film reviewing. Everyone knows the name Judith Crist, even if they don't know Susan Sontag, or even Renata Adler. Crist is the most influential film critic in the United States, according to the Harris Polls. In England the woman film reviewer Dilys Powell has attained such extraordinary popularity that she was awarded the title Commander of the British Empire in 1974, after 35 years of reviewing for the Sunday *Times.* Janet Maslin is presently reviewing for the *New York Times* (although clearly Vincent Canby gets first film choice) and seems well thought of by both other critics and her readership. Renata Adler put in a year of daily reviewing for the *New York Times* as well, with an unusually loyal audience, although her eclectic taste may not have been to everyone's liking. Adler's experiences at the *Times* are rather acerbically chronicled in her 1969 book *A Year in the Dark,* a collection of *Times* reviews. Adler reviewed briefly for *The New Yorker* in the fall of 1979.

Others—early and late—reviewed films, perhaps because initially film was considered of lesser importance than the drama (with of course a proportionately lower advertising revenue). Evelyn Gerstein wrote for major Boston daily newspapers and the *New Republic* in the 1920s and 1930s. In the same period, Velma Pilcher reviewed for *The Christian Science Monitor,* Helen Lawrenson for *Vanity Fair,* Cecilia Ager for *Vogue.* And in the 1950s and 1960s, Herminone R. Isaacs wrote a witty reviewing column for *Films in Review,* Moira Walsh a film column for the magazine *America,* and Claudia Cassidy—drama, music, and radio critic for the *Chicago Tribune* since the early-1940s—started reviewing films for *Chicago Magazine* in 1974, as well as doing film reviews for radio station WFMT. Kathleen Carroll has reviewed for the New York

Daily News since the early 1960s, and Judy Stone is the current film critic for the San Francisco *Chronicle* (and seems well-regarded in leftist circles).

Critics who review have often disparaged the practice, from Virginia Woolf to Renata Adler. Like novelists who complain in the old saw that journalism can destroy a writer (despite the outstanding examples to the contrary), they perceive reviewing as a stultifying craft. Or, like Adler and critic Malcolm Muggeridge in his *Chronicles of Wasted Time*, complain that the cinema does not have the intellectual solidity needed to withstand critical inquiry. Still others like David Denby contend that it is within the journalistic format that the best film criticism has been written.[1]

But for present-day reviewers who have so far achieved the greatest primacy their most important qualities are their quotability, readability, and consistency. Judith Crist, who has won any number of journalism awards for critical writing and has been film critic for the New York *Herald Tribune, New York* magazine, *Saturday Review,* and the "Today" show, trained to be a working journalist. Crist, who prefers to be referred to in print as Mrs. Crist, has a B.A. from Hunter College and a master's degree from Columbia University School of Journalism. She began her career as a reporter for the *Herald Tribune* in 1945, and eventually worked her way onto the arts page, serving as both drama and film critic. But despite her popularity and the financial success she earned from various syndicated columns, Crist's career has been not unmarked by either professional difficulties or criticisms. For many, she is a joke because she writes so many positive reviews that her laudatory blurbs and quotes can be seen on many marquees and in many newspaper ads at any one time. Crist was fired from the "Today" show, it is said, for duplicating fellow reviewer Gene Shalit's reviews. And she was also dropped from *New York* magazine in 1975, for which she had reviewed since 1968. Still, as of this writing, Crist continues to review for *T.V. Guide,* for which she has written since 1965, and for *The Washingtonian, Palm Springs Life,* and TV station WOR. The reviews are collected in *The Private Eye, the Cowboy, and the Very Naked Girl* (1968), and in *TV Guide to the Movies* (1974). And while she has sometimes been an object of derision in certain critical circles Crist is nonetheless included in the yearly anthology of the National Society of Film Critics, the collection of the best reviews and critical essays of that particular year. (In a possibly double-edged compliment, Pauline Kael has called Crist "the only film critic with balls.")

It is certainly true that Crist's critical standards are well nigh impossible to find, or define, and that much of her writing is cliché-ridden. In a "10 Best" piece for the New York *Herald Tribune* written in December 1964, Crist, like many others, liked director Stanley Kubrick's *Dr.*

Strangelove, Or: How I Learned to Stop Worrying and Love the Bomb.
She calls it a "masterpiece of movie-making of a very American kind."
But Crist doesn't explain what exactly an "American kind" means. Too,
the script, performances, and cinematic techniques are "superb," but we
don't find out how or why. Her praise of the 1973 film *Paper Moon* is
unexplained as well; it is shot in "beautiful, relaxing and appropriate
black and white" (*New York*, May 21, 1973). As it happens, we can discern that black and white may be appropriate for a film about the Depression, but Crist doesn't make that connection for us. Nor does she
say how and why a "non-color" film may be either beautiful or relaxing,
an idea that may be addressed in a short review, as work by others
shows.

Crist may be so popular, and so widely quoted, because she has this
very ability to slangily toss together some phrases that when closely
examined may make no logical sense but that on a fast read seem insigh-
ful. Alliteration helps. There is, for instance, a review of the 1964 *Dr.
Strangelove* that discusses Kubrick as satirically, mercilessly effective
in "parody and pastiche" (collected in *The Private Eye, the Cowboy, and
the Very Naked Girl*). *The Sting*, reviewed in the December 3, 1973 *New
York*, has "lush loot" although *Annie* is "lavish, literate, and . . . lovable" (*Saturday Review*, June 1982). Clearly unintentional hackneyed
phrases slip in as well; it's easy for a reader to quickly slide over them,
too. Nonmeaning and frequent clichés may "pass" on a rapid read.
Slaughterhouse Five is a "testament to the art of filmmaking"; it has
come to the screen with "a throbbing cinematic pulse" (*New York*, April
13, 1972). Of *Dead Men Don't Wear Plaid* Crist decides the movie is
"elegantly costumed and set in period" and—up pops this phrase
again—"appropriately filmed in black and white" (*Saturday Review*,
June 1982).

Crist's review of *Paper Moon* is a good example of why her work is
fitting for a readership intent upon knowing what a film is "about." It
also tells us what's wrong with her writing from the point of view of
more intellectually ambitious criticism. Three of the paragraphs of this
six-paragraph review of the 1973 film are devoted to a plot summary
and description of the characters' appearance, even of specific lines of
dialogue (used not to make a point about the character speaking them,
or the script, but simply to indicate what's going on). After reading a
Crist review, there can be no real surprises to the film, but this may be
exactly what some of her readers want. Little attempt is made to describe the visual qualities of a movie, except for what characters wear.
Tatum O'Neal has a "hideous cloche"; in the review of another film Elizabeth Taylor is "at her sun-tanned most *zahftig* effulgence, draped from
head-to-toe in wind-lashed chiffons" (*The Detective*, reviewed in *New
York* magazine, June 3, 1968). Only periodically does Crist mention the

cinematographer, and—almost never—the screenwriter. Insofar as she adopts any critical stance whatsoever, Crist must be said to be completely an auteurist critic.

Perhaps her lack of an aesthetic is just as well, for when Crist tries for a deeper critical analysis, things go sophomorically awry. In a review of Robert Altman's *Images,* Crist declares that these days "when the least of movies is more often than not beautifully photographed, I hasten to note that cinematographer Vilmos Zsigmond has attained the exquisite" (*New York,* October 9, 1972). Exquisite is a favorite Crist word.

It may simply be that mass readership is not interested in an analysis of the various elements of a working script or compositional technique and prefers the kind of snappy approach that can begin a review with a phrase like "Step aside, Sam, it's odious-comparison time" ("The Cream of the Year's Crop," New York *Herald Tribune,* December 27, 1964) or "Well, you asked for it, all you unsexhappy moviegoers, you, yearning for a family-type film" (*New York,* May 27, 1968, in a review of three French films). A fast read is the ticket here. And for a tired businessperson looking for a fast guide to an evening's entertainment, it's often perfect.

Besides, Crist seems to uncannily reflect middlebrow taste. This is definitely what has made her so commercially attractive to newspaper and magazine publishers. She prefers a film that is a "movie kind of movie, old-fashioned in the best sense," a film that is "meaningful rather than metaphorical." She snickers at those she calls "cinéastes," who look for—according to Crist—more in a film than might be there. What she likes about *Slaughterhouse Five* is that it unabashedly presents the "innocence that was once sincerely ours."

Some have claimed that Crist is a bit of a sexist, for she clearly doesn't mind a queen bee put-down or two of other women. In a review of *Thérèse and Isabelle* (*New York,* June 3, 1968), Crist wonders why anyone would enjoy watching a love affair between "two rather flat-chested ladies (no schoolgirls they, but pushing thirty, from the set of their hips)." And while in describing Tatum O'Neal's part in *Paper Moon* she may not be reactionary, Crist is quite resignedly traditional; one sees of Addie Pray that "in eternal woman fashion, she's up against a total stinker."

Yet Crist can manage to cut through a lot of pretentiousness at times, as her review of Sidney Lumet's *Serpico* shows. Of course Crist is commenting here, as usual, on the content of the film (in this fashion she often seems, in a burlesque of other women film critics, to confuse the film, and the actors, with "real" life and people). In a Greenwich Village party filled with "would-be" writers, artists, etc., who are "actually" working as admen, clerks, etc., Al Pacino's Serpico is at least working at what he really wants to do, and be. She admires the honesty of the character Pacino portrays, particularly in our "post-Watergate sickness. Let others buy the Sam Ervin bromides at 33 RPM; it's the Serpicos—and the price they have paid—who might inspire us to save ourselves" (*New York,* December 19, 1973). While not quite an Archie Bunker mentality, Crist, socially and politically, is often very middle-American. And much to her credit and in the national vein, completely unsnobbish.

It is perhaps Crist's lack of pretense and her ability to cut through hokum that she shares with Britain's much-loved and well-known woman film critic, Dilys Powell. Powell has been film critic for the Sunday *London Times* since 1939. Like Crist, she worked on the editorial staff of the paper for a while (from 1928–31 and from 1936–41). A graduate of Oxford College, twice married, and the author of a number of travel books and a biography, she took the years 1931–36 away from her job at the *Times* to work for the cause of Greek independence. Unlike Crist, Powell has written for more "serious" magazines and journals too, such as *Sight and Sound.* And her shorter reviews reveal a more comprehensive and deeper critical approach than Crist's. In an October 20, 1957 review of Elia Kazan's *A Face in the Crowd* the film is revealingly compared to Charlie Chaplin's *A King in New York,* and she devotes most of her piece to analyzing the two socially critical 1957 films. Powell is aware of dialogue; it is "harsh, exciting, sardonic" in Budd Schulberg's script for *A Face in the Crowd.* And she understands how dialogue is to be used, for we need to have it broken up so it isn't "wasted since the peculiar properties of the cinema make us so quickly tire of simply listening."

With some very fine writing, Powell decides that *A Face in the Crowd* is one of the "few genuinely political assaults the cinema has made. . . . It savages. It explodes; it is the guided missile." Chaplin's film shows to disadvantage next to Kazan's: the former has an "awkward jolt in the middle," but Kazan's film "changes trains almost imperceptibly." Frequently Powell integrates an awareness of structure into "think pieces," even reviews—a nice trick. She notes too that *A Face in the Crowd* is incredibly dense with "richness of detail." So that "even the restless individual movements which go to make up a crowd are closely observed." But, importantly, "without losing the narrative drive."

And her writing is continually inventive but not overblown. *A King in New York* is "likeable, easy; it ambles, it is a buggy-ride." Powell can be sprightly without being self-consciously witty, as we see in a couple of pieces on the profession of criticism. In the magazine section of the *London Times,* Powell's article "On Having It All Ways" (January 1, 1961) cleverly strings together complaints from all her correspondents and decides on an "all-purpose review; something for everybody. It would tell a story, but the wrong one, thus spoiling nobody's fun. It would be committed, but to what nobody would be able to discover," and so on. And in this way no one would be offended. In a witty retrospective piece in the January 6, 1974 Sunday *Times,* after being awarded the title of Commander of the British Empire, Powell discusses the state of criticism as she remembers it when she began as a critic nearly 35 years before. Then, charmingly, self-depreciatingly, "Yes, I know that seems longer to some of you." And—despite her redoubtable position—Powell is not afraid to use colloquial diction such as "splendidly creepy" about Murnau's 1922 *Nosferatu.*

She is capable of some probing theoretical statements as well. In an article entitled "Colour and the Film" in *Sight and Sound* (summer 1946), Powell decides that color has emerged from the period when it was a "new trick"; something for the "groundlings." Nor is it any longer "hideous," substituting the "illusion of an animated Neapolitan ice" for the monochromatic film. In fact, with the 1944 Olivier film *Henry V* in mind, Powell recommends using color for a "narrative and emotional effect." The tones of Olivier's face at his nighttime camp scene are "dark and Rembrandtesque." And the "brilliant blues and yellows and scarlets of the morning French army heightened the sense of relief from vigil." Some of the scenes Powell cites—just two years after the Olivier film was released—are those that latter-day critics have seen as significant, so her critical judgments have withstood the test of time.

What Powell recommends is a "poetic" use of color as in the "under-water sequences in *Pinocchio,* the pink elephant sequences in *Dumbo.*" Two other films that she feels have done well with color are *Blood and Sand* and *Caesar and Cleopatra.* It is almost as if Powell were prophesying a future Antonioni, Bergman, or Bertolucci. And her grasp of narrative, dialogue, and rhythm as elements to be underscored by color give yet one more indication of Powell's comprehension of cinematic elements. Rather than approaching film completely from the outside, it is as though Powell were holding one of those paperweights filled with snow. She describes the details she sees, while looking *through* the object as well. Herein she radically differs from other more pedestrian reviewers.

Powell of course is not the only daily, or weekly, woman critic to integrate some more "difficult" ideas into her work. Renata Adler is another, whose training as a political reporter might automatically lead to a broader, or at least a different, perspective. Adler began her career as a book reviewer for *The New Yorker,* but became a political and cultural reporter, she has said in the introduction to her collection of *Times* film reviews, because "I do not believe in professional criticism anyway, as a way of life. I turned to reporting, and it seemed to make more sense" (*A Year in the Dark: Journal of a Film Critic, 1968–1969,* 1969).

And when in 1967 the *New York Times* "almost incidentally" offered her Bosley Crowther's job as film reviewer, Adler was not as opposed to it as she might have been had the position involved book reviewing. For reviewing movies was "like writing about events." Moreover, like most people, Adler had "always gone to the movies a lot and liked to go to them." And—in common with many critics and writers about the cinema—Adler makes the connection between going to the movies and dreaming. It later turned out, she reports, that her favorite screening time was during the morning hours when the transition from sleep was an easy one. Too, going to movies "so completely blotted out the content of much of my life, and yet filled the days, like dreaming."

In preparation for the job, Adler reports she spent a few months seeing every film possible and reading volumes of film criticism. She has some definite ideas about film criticism: her introduction to *A Year in the Dark* makes fun of the "giddy adjectivalists," the "brave commercialism deplorers," particularly—here she must have Pauline Kael in mind—the "angry trash claimers (writers who claim some movie they enjoyed is utter trash, and then become fiercely possessive about it)."

Adler was at the *New York Times* only 14 months, but the introduction to *A Year in the Dark* is filled with amusing anecdotes about the difficulties of meeting daily deadlines, or the pressures of being a *Times* reviewer at screenings (once Adler had to leave a screening midway through because of illness; nevertheless she was chastized by the film's distributor for her "gaffe"). Most of her complaints, however, center around the editing that her writing underwent at the *Times.* There was, according to Adler, a "continual leaning on sentences, cracking rhythms, questioning or crazily amplifying metaphors and allusions, on pieces that were not that good in the first place." A phrase like "unavailing work" became "unavailable work." Nora Sayre, also a *Times* reviewer, has said that it "just happened" that Adler was writing under a particularly autocratic editorial regime; when Sayre was writing for the *Times* changes in her prose were not that extreme and she only lost an occasional innuendo or witticism.[2]

Adler attracted an extremely loyal following. More than a decade later people still refer to her stint as a *Times* reviewer with some awe. An Adler review is always a surprise, for she is as unpredictable in her rationale for liking a film as for dismissing it. At its best her criticism is brilliantly iconoclastic and at its worst, irritable, even cranky. Perhaps most impressive, however, is that she can display a sense of perspective *at the moment* that is rare in daily, or even weekly, reviewers.

In 1968 nearly everyone was ebullient about *The Graduate;* typical is Crist's declaration that it is "seriocomic satire at its best." (For Bosley Crowther in the *Times,* it is "one of the best seriocomic social satires.") In retrospect it is refreshing to read a piece like Adler's that immediately saw both the strong and the weak points of the film. Adler cuts through a lot of the hullabaloo, particularly the symbol-analyzing, about the film. The movie, she declares, is "brilliant," if "rather unstable." *The Graduate* is like having one's most intelligent friend to dinner, watching him become more "witty and animated" with each moment, and then realizing he may be having a nervous breakdown. It is as if the "screenplay had lost its mind." For one thing, the film gets out of kilter because it starts to identify too much with Benjamin, the title character, and thus loses perspective.

One of its implausibilities is the sudden presentation of Mrs. Robinson as a "villainess" midway through the film and after the seduction of Benjamin has taken place (*New York Times,* February 11, 1968). From femme fatale she suddenly becomes ogre trying to separate young lovers. Adler is the first critic to note this unsupported change, and it took more than ten years and an enlightened feminist perspective for other critics to observe the same thing and comment on the "unfairness" to the role of the older woman. While a number of other critics, such as Richard Schickel in *Life* and John Simon in *The New Leader,* saw the first half as superior to the second, none was as specific as Adler in finding the structural flaw in both the screenplay and in the development of character.

Adler was more skeptical, too, of Stanley Kubrick's *2001* than most, cleverly saying it looks like "the apotheosis of fantasy of a precious, early nineteen-fifties city boy." For although the film elicited a highly polarized response, the special effects were consistently praised. Adler, however, calls its visual pyrotechnics "self-absorbed," the "visual equivalent of rubbing the stomach and patting the head" (*New York Times,* April 4, 1968).

Just so, Adler's *New Yorker* review of *Breaking Away* takes us pleasantly unaware (Adler pinch-hit for a time during Kael's absence). She uses this universally liked, effective, unpretentious film, to decide— if a bit elliptically—that the audience's frequent applause at the end of the film has to do almost with relief. For once, no major critical issue is at stake in the viewing of a film. It is here, Adler declares, that we can see how the focus of attention in the cinema has shifted, almost by decades, from the stars to the film maker to criticism itself. This shift, Adler asserts rather originally, exists in no other field. The critic, in film, is not a commentator but a protagonist in a drama "to which the work under review serves as a gloss." And of course viewers these days see themselves as critics. Since *Breaking Away* raises no major critical concerns, people are released from a certain burden; advance publicity has informed them, Adler tells us, that they will not have to take a stand. It is quite a clever idea to take this tack, as so many lavishly praised the film with oft-repeated phrases about "refreshing" qualities that by the time the weekly *New Yorker* came out readers may have been ready for something else.

Some of Adler's own ambivalence about film, and about reviewing, comes to the fore in the *Breaking Away* piece. She decides that "most movies simply will not support much criticism" so the "vitality and conviction of a practicing critic" are "almost certain to exceed those of most films" (*The New Yorker,* November 5, 1979). Still, Adler sometimes sees some of the finer possibilities for criticism, deciding that the moment a reviewer exists for is when he notices something that "might otherwise have just gone by. It is like a little, recognizing wave of the hand" ("On Reviewing, II: A Wayne Sympathetic Frame of Mind," *New York Times,* December 1, 1968). In typical Adler fashion she has begun by disclaiming the whole business of writing about reviewing. "On Reviewing, I: Turnstiles" starts in a similar fashion. Reviews are just "endorsements, opinions, insult controversy, de facto controversy" in general, much overrated. Even so, a mixed review has a purpose: it "should serve as a turnstile which brings each reader to the kind of movie he would want to see," *New York Times,* March 17, 1968). Facet glimpsing yields an individual purity to criticism, even if it can preclude a solid critical stance.

Adler is a consistently clever, professional, writer. (She has written short stories for *The New Yorker* since 1962, and a novel, *Speedboat* was published in 1976.) A character in a Fassbinder film personifies a "sort of rococo Mother Courage." According to Adler, as a director, Fassbinder often churns out his melodramatic scenes with a "Muzak quality of indifference." But her barbs don't sting just for the sake of puncturing, like those of a critic such as John Simon. More frequently they indicate precisely what's wrong with a film. Mark Rydell, the director of *The Rose,* "has made, among other key miscalculations, the mistake of trying for a wall-to-wall finale" (*The New Yorker,* November 12, 1979). *Petulia* was a "nervous little film" using "jaggedly cutting," though Adler admits that the fragmentary snippets are remarkable for revealing a great deal about the characters (June 11, 1968). "Jaggedly" is deftly used next to "cutting," and here she beats even Pauline Kael's "glittering mosaic" for the film's editing style.

Probably Adler's greatest critical talent is her ability to zero in on the cultural detail of a film that tells much about either a character or the world view of a film. Adler says that John Cassavetes's *Faces* has a wonderfully revealing, repeated use of nervous laughter throughout which "cracks open now and then to tell more about America than any other movie in a long time" (*New York Times*, February 18, 1968). The recognizability, the mimetic qualities, of some scenes turns her on, too. Rather than the sci-fi or fantastic elements, what Adler does like about *2001* is its attention to "the almost cosmic boredom of space travel" that reminds her so much of the exhaustion, almost nausea, that travelers sometimes feel. Here she responds to the "human element"—to the faces—and in this fashion her piece may be tellingly compared to Andrew Sarris's review of the film in the *Village Voice* which ignores faces in favor of sci-fi phenomena.

Adler makes use of just the kind of opinionated "intrusion" that the current *New York Times* critic Janet Maslin generally omits from her reviews. Maslin has said that she believes in a "direct response to things" in her reviews, keeping as "little between me and the subject matter as possible."[3] Moreover, Maslin says that theory "can get in the way of a direct response to things."

Maslin's antipathy to a rigid application of theory (and her ability to still use whatever insights such a theory can provide) can be seen in an essay titled "Hollywood Heroines Under the Influence: Alice Still Lives Here" (*The Boston Phoenix*, February 25, 1975). While taking issue with what she sees as the phony self-conscious feminism displayed in *Alice Doesn't Live Here Anymore* and John Cassavetes's *A Woman Under the Influence*, both made in 1974, Maslin first argues that just because a film centers on a female character, it is no reason to assume that the film is a feminist tract. Yet she is quick to say in this article that "I don't like these films' assumptions that their heroines' resources are so meager; I don't like the way both women ultimately toss in the towel and are still somehow commended for their courage." Of course Maslin's piece is not the first to spot such inconsistencies, especially in the conclusion to Scorcese's *Alice Doesn't Live Here Anymore*. Molly Haskell makes a similar point in a *Village Voice* review of *Alice* (January 13, 1975), declaring that Kris Kristofferson's David saying "please" (stay on the ranch with me instead of pursuing your career) to Alice allows her to keep both her dream and her dignity.

Yet Maslin's flexibility—which does allow her to cut in a number of directions—also makes it difficult to determine her exact stance when Kristofferson gets angry with Alice. Maslin defends him by saying he's only "gotten tough with her, in a way that director Scorcese who handles Alice lovingly but much too gingerly throughout—should have attempted to himself." This rather indiscriminate meld of director, actor, and actress is typical of the kind of passionate loss of perspective we have seen in the work of other women film critics. Instead, in Vincent Canby's review of the same film in the *New York Times*, we see a very clear distinction maintained between actor and director: "It's Miss Burstyn's movie and part of the enjoyment of the film is the director's apparent awareness of this fact, as in a sequence in which Alice is making a little extra money by singing and playing ersatz cocktail piano in a roadside tavern."

Maslin had been a math major at the University of Rochester, where she specialized in computer science. Not liking the extremely competitive atmosphere, she went to Boston where she became a secretary at Harvard and started writing on rock and roll for *The Phoenix*, an alternative newspaper. In 1971 she switched to film, when a reviewer who had "been possessive of" film finally left. Maslin had reviewed for a year for *Newsweek*, where her prose was "heavily edited," when she was hired by the *Times* in 1977.[4] She also wrote for *New Times*. Maslin reviews an average of about four films a week for the *New York Times*, although she may see as many as 20, she has said. Occasionally, she reviews television and records too. Having written about various forms, she says she decided that film critics in particular are an odd bunch, in that "it's very satisfying to be both immediately involved and yet removed." For the reviewer can feel "part of" film, in that film viewing is projective, yet avoids the responsibility of judging the live actor on stage.

One of the best things about Maslin's prose is that she is an easy read, while still maintaining a high level of literacy, especially when compared to a writer like Judith Crist. In Maslin's review of *The Seduction of Joe Tynan*, she decides that "Rip Torn brings a new dimension to political sleaziness in the role of skirt-chasing (and catching)." And Melvyn Douglas is "suitably alarming" as an elder statesman on the "verge of senility" (August 17, 1979). The film *Foxes* has a wonderfully phrased "melting glamour" that could "smooth its way into the first Los Angeles *Nouvelle Vague* Film Festival" (February 29, 1980).

A review of director Ted Kotcheff's 1979 *North Dallas Forty*, a football film, more punnily sees that the hero's best friend is that only up to the point when self-interest "is called into play, in which case all bets are off." And once in a while, as in this review, Maslin can "descend" to the kind of corniness that seems to come under the pressures of daily reviewing. Getting the hero through a football game requires "drugs, tape, padding and possibly the odd dash of papier-maché or Krazy Glue" (August 1, 1979). An unfortunate propensity for low-level humor can be observed in a "think piece" about the same film, that an early party sequence "makes *Animal House* look like *Animal Nursery School*" ("Two That Bolt Their Genres," about *North Dallas Forty* and

Clint Eastwood's *Escape From Alcatraz,* August 5, 1979).

In contrast to a review like Renata Adler's of *Breaking Away,* Maslin places that film in the context of the year's formulaic films— "unknown boxer/bowler/jogger hopes to become sports hero"—and then descriptively declares it to be "so fresh and funny it didn't even need a big budget or pedigree." Yet another reason why it is in the classic "sleeper" category is its setting in Bloomington, Indiana, perhaps "the world's equivalent of left field." And she picks some of the film's most amusing moments to describe, as well as setting forth a number of the better lines of dialogue, like Indiana father Paul Dooley's complaints about the Italian turn his family cuisine has taken: "All them 'ini' foods, zucchini and linguini and fettucine." But she, unfortunately, ends the piece with an unsubtle witticism that although Paul Dooley's character doesn't know it yet, by the end of the story he'll be "eating pizza." (Italian things are a symbol for the more fanciful—and not-Midwestern—lifestyle that hero Dave, Dennis Christopher and his mother, Barbara Barrie, are attracted to).

Still, a review like Maslin's of Diane Kury's film *Peppermint Soda,* while perhaps omitting some of the film's finely observed bits about sibling rivalry—directly captures the film's charm, its "flair for taking things absolutely seriously while never forgetting to take them lightly, too" (July 15, 1979). Here Maslin exhibits perhaps her best talent: an ability to catch the multiplicity, the richness of detail inherent in film that we have seen in the work of other women film critics. However, occasionally, like Penelope Houston, she tends to get too caught up in describing minor elements. It may be perfectly fitting for Maslin to observe that the teenage heroine "has a boyfriend, whose letters Anne routinely steams open." This speaks to the theme of sisterhood. But we probably *don't* need to know the extraneous detail that their "gym teacher wears a fur coat while the girls are outdoors in shorts," or that the art teacher picks on her students as they "sketch a little statuette of Bambi."

Of course some of the perspective that is lacking in a daily review is seen in an essay on *The Great Gatsby* where Maslin compares it to *Gone With the Wind:* "both books understand that the eroticism of wealth is a crucial ingredient in American daydreams about love and seduction" (in *The Classic American Novel and the Movies,* Peary and Shatzkin, eds. New York: Ungar, 1977). And it's to be found in a Sunday "essay" like Maslin's on *Breaking Away* and *Peppermint Soda,* "The Best Years of Our Lives? Two Views of Adolescence." Here, more depth is possible. In this essay Maslin is able to capture a fine sense of generation. Paul Dooley "feels just as much like a pariah at the University of Indiana [sic] as his son does, even though he helped build the place." And Maslin finds a nice phrase for the "paralyzing passivity that the town's caste system threatens to impose." She discovers a revealing, feminist comparison between the two different sexes' versions of adolescence: "The girls in *Peppermint Soda*, being much younger, are more concerned with matters of authority than these boys, and less sure of what to do with power on those rare occasions when they have it" (July 29, 1979).

Yet while a piece like "Two That Bolt Their Genres: *North Dallas Forty* and *Escape From Alcatraz*" has a built-in organizing idea or thesis, a Sunday *Times*, Arts and Leisure "Film View" that discusses *All That Jazz* and *Apocalypse Now* flounders as it tries to find the same merits and flaws in these two "huge, sprawling, expensive curiosities" (*Times*, January 13, 1980). There may be a connective link between these films, but it certainly isn't that we can dismiss their faults because they try to do too much. There are no startling hook-ups here, which of course may be just what the *New York Times* in the late-1970s and early-1980s wants. Even a piece that discusses the "effectiveness" of the obscene or off-color language used in recent films comes across as rather bland and slightly reactionary. After saying that while harsh language "can serve a positive purpose," Maslin qualifies this by deciding that movies can "supply their characters with offensive dialogue without resorting to the standard obscenities at all," just as they did "in the good old days" ("Just A Matter of Taste?" *New York Times*, August 12, 1979). Maslin may turn out to be an undistinguished reviewer after all: thorough and responsible but a feminist Uncle Tom.

It is easy to disparage reviewing as ephemeral or as a craft.[5] Or it may be seen as merely a cultural indicator as in a comparison of Adler's 1960s and Maslin's 1970s *Times* reviews. Clearly, reviewing has more than just an informational function, since so many different styles and methods of attack are possible within this form. This in fact may be the real reason women have been drawn to reviewing. It is a free form enough—still—for them to knock into some shape of their own. Maslin may spend a great deal of time discussing why *Peppermint Soda* reminds her of her youth, Adler may take an entire reviewing space to tell us why *Breaking Away* inspires a noncritical response, and spend little time on the film. Judith Crist is able to take off on a tangent about lost values. (And even so we may see women critics' affinities for detail, for personalizing, for mimetic tangibility.)

For even within the framework of deadline meeting, editor pleasing, space considerations, and a taboo of revealing a plot device, reviewing is perhaps the least codified of all the critical forms, especially since the advent of the new journalism with the possibility for autobiographical intrusions and literary flourishes. Unlike the essay or book, there is nothing that must be proven. The writer is released from the burdens—as well as the intellectual impact—of the "thesis." Floating around in the space and time of often not entirely linear thought, the review may just be the form most analogous to the cinema.

NOTES

1. See Denby's introduction to *Awake in the Dark* (New York: Vintage/Random House, 1973).

2. Interview, New York City, January 3, 1980.

3. Interview, New York City, May 21, 1979. All subsequent Maslin quotes refer to this interview.

4. It is an interesting aside that many journalistic film reviewers disclaim actively seeking their job. Nora Sayre has said the offer to review for the *Times* "blew in the window." Janet Maslin declared she has always been passive when it came to finding a reviewing position. And Renata Adler, as we have seen, has said that the job was offered to her "almost incidentally." Perhaps it is just a standard journalistic ploy to discredit effort. Helen Lawrenson has said in *Stranger at the Party* (1973) that the first thing she learned in becoming a journalist was to appear as if she weren't working hard.

5. See especially Virginia Woolf's essay, "Reviewing," in *The Captain's Death Bed and Other Essays* (New York: Harcourt, Brace, 1950).

5

The Theorists:

Susan Sontag, Annette Michelson, Maya Deren, Hortense Powdermaker, and Claude-Edmonde Magny

There are five women writers who have ventured into the difficult arena of "serious" film theory. For three of them—French critic Claude-Edmonde Magny, avant-garde film maker Maya Deren, and anthropologist Hortense Powdermaker—their theoretical writing on film is an interesting sidestep to their main careers. But for the other two—the universally acclaimed critic of nearly every phase of the arts, novelist and screenwriter Susan Sontag, and former art critic and current professor of cinema studies at New York University, Annette Michelson—it is their criticism, and their theoretical statements that have made the strongest mark. Even defining theory in the loosest possible way, it is difficult to imagine under what possible common umbrella these five disparate intellectuals could possibly shelter. Yet as women critics of the cinema they do share surprisingly common ground. Magny is one of the first serious critics to propose a theory integrating physical details and the "star" personality. She, Powdermaker, and Deren all freely employ the dream metaphor, and everything that it implies, and Sontag emphasizes as well the vicarious nature of the cinema "experience."

Perhaps more than any other critic, however, it is Susan Sontag who "makes use of" the special properties of film to support some of her cultural generalizations, particularly in her extraordinarily influential and popular collection of essays *Against Interpretation* which took— and, most significantly, made—a position on the arts that seemed for most people to define the 1960s sensibility—that period generally thought of now as one of "cultural explosion" in the arts. *Against Interpretation*, which was nominated for a National Book Award and created a sensation among critics, calls for rather than a "hermeneutics," an "erotics" of art, and boldly brushes aside former aesthetic theories like the mimetic in order to assert the values of "sensual immediacy" over "meaning" in art. The films of Robert Bresson, of Godard, and Resnais, which Sontag speaks of in this volume, are ideal works on which to build a theory of "self-reflexive" art. Sontag also treats Bergman as well as Godard in the later collection *Styles of Radical Will;* included is a long piece comparing the theater and film.

Sontag, born to a middle-class family in 1933, divides her time between New York City and Paris. She has degrees from the University of Chicago (a B.A. was earned at nineteen) and Harvard. She slyly disavows her critical abilities, claiming that her criticism has been merely a "case study" for explaining her own taste in postabstract painting, the French antinovel, and avant-garde and underground movies. Even her most well-known, if not most highly regarded essay, "Notes on Camp," an unusually structured and cleverly written article of 49 short notes or paragraphs that defined the "camp" sensibility of the 1960s and that moved Sontag into the realm of popular media attention, is passed off as a working out of a personal aesthetic. (One of the interesting aspects of her criticism is the form of a philosophic "proof" that some of her criticism takes, most evident in the numbered listing of her arguments as she does in her work on Godard or in "Notes on Camp." Sontag—trained and published as a philospher—is one of the few women critics to transfer this format to film criticism.) Nor, she claims, does she seek attention for her work; the introduction to *Against Interpretation* disarmingly worries how a "bulky essay in the *Partisan Review* could be turned into a trendy catch-phrase in *Newsweek.*"

Sontag sometimes bills herself as a novelist (*The Benefactor* was published in 1963 and *Death Kit* in 1967) and film maker (she wrote and directed *Duet for Cannibals* in 1969 and did the screenplay for *Brother Carl* in 1972) and has said in an interview that "I don't consider that I ever was a critic. I had ideas, and I attached them to works of art that I admired. Now I attach them to other things" (*Performing Arts Journal,* fall 1977). Yet her essays—originally published in journals and periodicals such as *Film Quarterly, The Nation,* the *New York Review of Books,* and *Partisan Review*—have been numerous enough to be collected in *Against Interpretation* (1966), *Styles of Radical Will* (1969), and *Under the Sign of Saturn* in 1980. She seems to have changed her tack (not an unusual Sontag ploy, as we will see) that in many ways film making is preferable to writing: "The film thing is tremendously seductive. The simple pleasure of working with people. Writing is such an ascetic, solitary occupation. You can get hooked—as I am—on the fun of making films" (*New York Times,* October 3, 1969). Sontag's book *On Photography* came out in 1977 and *Illness as a Metaphor* in 1980 after her successful battle against cancer.

It meant a great deal for the erudite Sontag—whose detractors concede to be brilliantly persuasive even if they feel wrong-headed—to declare in the 1964 essay that keynoted the volume *Against Interpretation* that the elusive quality of art is what makes it "good," and that this is why the cinema is "the most alive, the most exciting, the most important of all art forms right now." This assertion is based on the fact that the cinema has a surface "so unified and clean, whose momentum is so rapid, whose address is so direct that the work can be . . . just what it is." Robert Bresson's films, which are more often glowingly described than analyzed, are perfect examples of this type of cinematic aesthetic, according to Sontag.

She even goes so far as to say that one way to tell how vital an art form is may be by determining how much "latitude it gives for making mistakes in it, and still being good." This is one of those conjectures that would seem outrageous if advanced by someone else, yet Sontag can quite successfully get away with it. One example is Bergman, whose ideas, according to her, may be "lame" although the films still triumph. Another example comes from the works of D.W. Griffith in whose work "beauty and visual sophistication of the images subvert before our eyes the callow pseudo-intellectuality of the story."

Sontag's aphoristic style is at its best piercing in its self-contained brilliance and at its worst is a conundrum of unexplained ideas, interesting though each may be in its own right. Transparence, she decides, is the "highest, most liberating value of art—and in criticism—today." Specifically, it is in the films of Japanese director Ozu, and in Renoir's *Rules of the Game,* that we can experience the "luminousness of the thing in itself, of things being what they are." Another example is Hans-Jurgen Syberberg's seven-hour epic *Hitler, A Film From Germany,* which is a "mosaic of stylistic quotations" (*New York Review of Books,* February 21, 1980). Even more specifically, Sontag begins her piece on Syberberg with one of those breathtakingly original and witty remarks that seem unassailable and make us wonder why such an obvious point hadn't been made, and grasped, before: "Where so many blandishments flourish," Sontag decides, "bringing off a masterpiece seems a retrograde feat, a naive form of accomplishment. Always rare, the Great Work is now truly odd." Another essay starts with the observation that in art, as in life, there are husband and lovers. And one shouldn't have to do without either. Witty descriptions are sprinkled throughout Sontag's prose: even as German film maker Leni Riefenstahl gets older, photographs show her to have a "gay, metallic quality" ("Fascinating Fascism," *New York Review of Books,* February 6, 1975).

In a yin-yang approach to film criticism, critics Sontag likes are those who "reveal the sensuous surface of art without mucking about in it" who will therefore be able to give us back our "sensory experience of the work of art" ("Against Interpretation"). But it is true that her own criticism often employs instead the kind of analytical method she is here taking to task. In a clever—probably tongue-in-cheek—essay that dissects the component parts of the science fiction film, "The Imagination of Disaster," Sontag finds the formula consisting of a number of elements like the "arrival of the thing," and "further atrocities." Moreover, the science fiction film is not about science, but about disaster, one of the oldest subjects of art. Yet the visual elements are still emphasized; it is "in the imagery of destruction that the core of a good science fiction film lies." Science fiction is also morally simplistic, an insight that will be repeated by later critics.

The piece that perhaps most exemplifies Sontag's cinema aesthetic and "radically chic" stance is a review of a pop pornographic film, Jack Smith's *Flaming Creatures*, which first appeared in *The Nation* on April 13, 1964 and caused a bit of a furor. The 1964 film—which had difficulty in the courts—makes use of gigantically enlarged genital images as well as references to nostalgia favorites like Irene Dunne and Yvonne de Carlo. Although it is about a "transvestite orgy," Sontag feels that the film is not pornographic since the images of sex are alternately childlike and witty." However, it *is* in the "poetic cinema of shock"—in particular the "poetry of transvestism." It is interesting in this context to compare Sontag's more off-handed remarks about pornography in her 1977 book *On Photography*. "Images anesthetize," Sontag declares (not a brand new insight), and so therefore the shock of a pornographic movie wears off.

But in *Flaming Creatures*, the visions of "shaken breast and the shaken penis" become interchangeable, making them prime candidates for the kind of image that is often found in pop art and that is not reducible to anything else. Therefore it is perfect for Sontag's aesthetic, and a "triumphant example of an aesthetic vision of the world—and such a vision is perhaps always, at its core, epicene." This rather elliptical logic that a pure vision is epicene, or androgynous, is not explained however, and Sontag concludes this thought, and the piece, with a somewhat elitist message: that "this type of art has yet to be understood in this country" (the United States), for it "dwells in aesthetic—not moral space." It is easy to see here why she may be irritating to nonelitist critics, especially those like Pauline Kael who emphasize narrative and moral or sociological significance. Kael punctures this essay of Sontag's nicely: "in treating indiscriminateness as a value, Miss Sontag has become a real swinger. Of course, we can reply that if anything goes, nothing happens, nothing works" ("Are Movies Going to Pieces?") the *Atlantic Monthly*, December 1964).

It is not an unusual critical ploy to take a little known and/or lightly regarded work and make an aesthetic case for it, as Sontag is doing with *Flaming Creatures*. This is often true of Sontag, who seems to delight in revealing facets of work that haven't been shown before.

Not perverse or truly eclectic, but chameleon-like, Sontag can fine-tune in to the culture. She can even, in fact, flip-flop or waffle on a certain position. Perhaps the most well-known example of this tendency is her stance on Leni Riefenstahl's *Triumph of the Will* and *Olympiad*, films that project "grace and sensuousness" in 1965 for Sontag, but that cannot be seen outside of the context of their "propaganda" in 1980.

Even so, Sontag manages to work Reifenstahl into her overall film aesthetic. Her often-anthologized piece "Fascinating Fascism," which first appeared in the February 6, 1975 *New York Review of Books*, takes its flashy title from its sensationalistic subjects. In the piece, Sontag reviews two books published in 1974, *The Last of the Nuba* by Leni Reifenstahl, a book of photographs by the film maker and photograper, and *S.S. Regalia* by Jack Pia, a lightweight book examining the costumes of the Nazis. The main thrust, however, is on the increasingly positive reputation of Reifenstahl who made *Triumph of the Will* with the complete cooperation of Hitler, which Sontag quite properly does not let us forget. (The cult for Reifenstahl, despite her shady ideological background, is explained by Sontag: feminists "would feel a pang at having to sacrifice the one woman who made films that everybody acknowledges to be first-rate." She is, only too obviously, the only woman director Sontag has chosen to deal with. No strained feminist rediscoveries necessary; and although the moral and aesthetic arguments may shift, Riefenstahl is a safe bet for critical longevity. See also, Andrew Sarris's sly recanting piece "The Ladies Auxiliary, 1976," written for the Kay and Peary collection *Women and the Cinema*.)

But the main reason we accept Riefenstahl's art as important is a "shift in taste which simply makes it impossible to reject art if it is 'beautiful.'" For if the message of fascism has been "neutralized by an aesthetic view of life, its trappings have been sexualized." While Sontag does not concentrate solely on the cinematic "found objects," there is still the emphasis on detail, on the "vast repertory of popular iconography usable for the ironic commentaries of Pop art." Less seriously, the symbols of Nazi "regalia" are just "sexier." And though it's quite rare for Sontag to stoop to such a tactic, she does in this case point out factual inaccuracies in the promotional information on the cover of Riefenstahl's book.

When she cavils, it is generally for other reasons. In her essay on Bergman's 1965 *Persona*, she finds the film to be a masterwork, but still quite effectively dismisses the rest of Bergman's opus. He has a "prodigal, tirelessly productive career" that is "rather facile" owing to a "lavishly inventive, sensual, yet melodramatic talent" that's prone to "embarrassing displays of intellectual bad taste." He is, in short, the "Fellini of the North."

She's as intent in praise, too. Godard is not "merely an intelligent iconoclast" but a "deliberate 'destroyer' of cinema" in his changing around of various cinematic structures (for instance, refusing to stick to one point of view). According to Sontag, the great cultural heroes of our time have shared two qualities: they have all been "ascetics in some exemplary way, and also great destroyers." It sometimes seems as if Sontag works by induction from very few, sometimes even one, example. First she offers the example-based insight and then moves right on to the culturally-important generalization. Hard to argue with, since at least the one example is self-evidently true.

She praises Godard for many reasons, however. Like Bresson, he is "consciously, even self-consciously reflective." And she responds positively to Godard's efforts in the direction of "synaesthesia"—the deliberate mixing of the arts. Here she freely draws from his statements in interviews and critical writing. The concept of synaesthesia is fully explained by Sontag in her long essay "Theatre and Film" where she divides and explains the two dominant critical approaches to the arts. "Consider," she says, "the two principal radical positions in the arts today. One recommends the breaking down of distinctions between genres; the arts would eventuate in one art." And the other position "recommends the maintaining and clarifying of barriers between the arts," so that "painting must use only those means which pertain to painting," for example. Sontag makes it clear, however, that it's the merging of the arts that she feels is the more interesting. (In this context the sci-fi genre piece appears to be a clever exercise.) A number of critics—André Bazin and George Bluestone are two—have made statements that tout the cross-fertilization of film and literature; Sontag, in common with other women film critics, seems much more in favor of a deliberate mix.

In the significant "Theatre and Film" Sontag touches on and summarizes most of the boundaries of the cinema theory that looks at film as a popular art, which in a "vaguely Marxist orientation" collaborates with a fundamental tenet of romanticism, the attempt to fix time. For the cinema is a "time machine," an automatically dated phenomenon that "freezes" certain images (a point made by critics early and late). It is not startling that Sontag would see the cinema as attractive to Marxists, nor is it an unusual insight to recognize that film, as originally a popular art form, would be susceptible to a philosophical school that sees the masses as the most important. But to wed this to the romantic hope for altering or stopping time—even in a critical overview—is a rather brilliant and unique connection. Sontag discusses the universally assented to temporal and "spatial" qualities of film, although she differentiates by saying that films don't *necessarily* [emphasis added] need to roam over space and time. The example is the Japanese film *The Lower Depths* (1959).

Some of Sontag's ideas may remind us of the critical notions of Annette Michelson, flamboyant teacher of avant-garde film criticism and theory at New York University. Sontag mentions, in the introduction to *Against Interpretation,* that Michelson has "shared her erudition and taste with me in many conversations over the last seven years," so this perhaps comes as no surprise. Close friends in Paris in the 1960s, it is now hinted in film criticism circles that Michelson is miffed at Sontag's popularity, which may have been based on the successful popularization of Michelson's ideas.

Michelson, whom film critic and archivist Jonas Mekas has called "the high priestess of the avant garde," was originally an art critic and art editor of the Paris *Tribune* in the 1950s. She returned to this country, it is reported she's said, in order to "straighten out" the state of film criticism. The author of a number of highly regarded essays in the highbrow journal *Artforum* (for which Michelson originally wrote art criticism, until "switching over" to film in the late-1960s), and in the journal *October,* founded in 1978, Michelson has been editor of both journals. She is generally credited with bringing attention and critical acclaim to experimental film maker Michael Snow, most known for his 1967 film *Wavelength.*

In her articles about Snow in *October,* Michelson insists on the formal, or self-contained, qualities of a film, although her criticism has a socially oriented, radical edge as well. For, one of her main contentions, as a Marxist critic, is that the American film industry took as its model the factory system of division of labor from the automotive industry. Directors therefore are no more than cogs in the wheel, so that each young person wishing to work in this medium has had to decide whether he or she wishes to direct films or to "really" make them. This argument is fully developed in an essay, "Paul Sharits and the Critique of Illusionism: An Introduction," from *Projected Images* (the catalogue to a show of four artists, one of whom was Paul Sharits, at the Walker Art Center in Minneapolis).

An even more explicitly leftist piece is "Film and the Radical Aspiration," originally published in 1966 and collected in the classic anthology about the avant-garde film, *Film Culture Reader* (1970). Michelson's contention is that after a moment of "consummation" between political and formal goals (read, perhaps, aesthetic ends) in the revolutionary Soviet film of the 1920s and early-1930s, the two impulses or trends split, so that political art became—in the modern tradition—a "formal statement of the impossibility of discourse." But there are possibilities breaking for politically and artistically unified films, for finally, today in America "our best independent film makers . . . are committed to an aesthetic of autonomy that by no means violates or excludes their critical view of the society in which they manage, as they can, to work."

This hopeful sense is encouraged by Michelson's concluding description of children, even within what she considers to be a repressive capitalistic system, making films in their own backyards. Film—as a subversive activity—can be open to all, even kids. But perhaps the best thing about this article, which takes as its subject the history of the avant-garde film, is a kind of cinematic "prehistory" that is one of the most stylistically elegant statements Michelson has made:

> Film, our most vivacious art, is young enough to remember its first dreams, its limitless promise, and it is haunted, scarred, by a central, ineradicable trauma of dissociation. The attendant guilt and ambivalence, their repressive effects, the manner above all, in which a dissociative principle has been alternately resisted or assumed, converted into an aesthetic principle, the manner in which this resistance or conversion modified or redefines cinematic aspirations are, like everything concerning film, unique in the history of Western culture.

The dream analogy is carried throughout the essay, and is as heavily relied upon by Michelson as by so many other women film critics.

Other pieces by Michelson touch on some of the themes Sontag has treated. In "About Snow" (*October,* spring 1979), she analyzes the mid-1960s interpenetration of the arts in an effort to explain the context in which Snow developed, and the increasing freedom with which methods and modes of visual perception could be played with—some critics feel permanently altered—by his films. Like the films of Stan Brakhage, who Michelson also admires and mentions in this article, these independent films aim toward new visions that are clearly nonlinear, or, as Michelson more creatively puts it, "vision uncorrupted by that Fall we know as the Renaissance, perpetuated by the codes of representation and ground into the very lenses of the camera." McLuhanesque notions about nonlinearity, simultaneity, and freedom from the tyranny of print hierarchy underlies much of this, but Michelson's training in art history is perhaps most relied upon in the frame-by-frame shot analysis exemplified by the photographs that accompany her articles.

One of the most ingenious of Michelson's articles is wittily titled "Bodies in Space: Film as 'Carnal Knowledge,'" which appeared in the February 1969 issue of *Artforum.* Here the entire film viewing experience transforms to metaphor, as the theatre seat becomes a space vessel, so that "one rediscovers, through the shock of recognition, one's own body living in *its* space." And beyond: through "acknowledgement of disorientation," things, "thanks to Kubrick," may never be the same "*in quite the same way.*" The hope for and the insistence on apocalyptic change that counterculture films and criticism often centered around may now seem overstated and naive. Michelson's method of dealing with the mixed critical reaction to *2001* is more ingenious. She implies that negative criticism may have come about because of the "clear projection of aging mind and bodies. Its hostile dismissal constitutes, rather like its timid defense, an expression of fatigue."

Michelson has written as persuasively—if a bit more traditionally—on the Soviet film makers Eisenstein and Vertov. Eisenstein is no new critical discovery, although Michelson adroitly demonstrates how Eisenstein's films take their shape from his philosophy. Vertov, she decides, is the maker of the greatest of the "city documentaries, *"The Man With the Movie Camera"* (1928), and in the "pioneer" category he is also the founder of a number of technical innovations. He was first to intrude animation techniques into the action in order to alternate slow and normal speeds, and—particularly important from the point of view of Michelson's aesthetics—Vertov "reminds" us of the presence of the screen as a surface. (Here we can spot some similarities between Michelson's and Sontag's ideas.) Quite cleverly, Michelson takes us back in time to look at a photograph of an All-Union Creative Conference of Workers in Soviet Cinema by imaginatively describing what the 1920s conference must have been like.

Michelson's detractors find her style to be far too obtuse for readability, or even comprehension. They see her logic as too elliptical and her references as elitist, even purposefully recondite. For instance, a description of a walk through a wax museum leads her to conclude that "as we went slowly through the long, dark, labyrinthian corridor, punctuated by the rather grand tableaux that chronicle the whole of French history, from the early Gauls until the Gaullist regime, [it seemed] that the wax museum, in its very special, hallucinatory darkness, its spatial ambiguity, its forcing of movement upon the spectator, its mixture of diversion and didacticism, is a kind of protocinema" ("Film and the Radical Aspiration"). Or they find her overly partisan as in her analogizing between Stan Brakhage and Sergei Eisenstein (particularly in "Camera Lucida/Camera Obscura," in *Artforum*, January 1973), or in her extreme, repeated, and undiluted praise of Michael Snow's work.

But all agree that Michelson can see things in the avant-garde film that others cannot. The introduction to P. Adams Sitney's *Film Culture Reader*, perhaps the bible of avant-garde film theory, seems pedestrian if soberly straightforward and responsible by comparison. It is clear too that Michelson's references derive from a fine critical understanding of the other arts; not just art history, but literature as well (although perhaps her piece on Brakhage and Eisenstein overuses T.S. Eliot's "Tradition and the Individual Talent"). And even if one is a Michelson aficionado it is sometimes difficult to bring her rarefied sensibility into line with her radical political, sometimes Marxist, stance.

Both Sontag and Michelson have incorporated their thoughts about the avant garde into their respective theoretical positions, and they contain, interestingly, elements both of elitism and of leftism while also reflecting their personal taste. Yet one of the very first explicators of the avant-garde film was Maya Deren, herself a film maker. Her most famous film is *Meshes of the Afternoon*, made in 1943, in which a woman's dream becomes so intense it achieves near reality. Dubbed the "mother of us all" by Jonas Mekas, also an independent film maker, Deren's films include *At Land* (1944), *The Very Eye of Night* (1959), *Ritual in Transfigured Time* (1945), and *Witches Cradle* (1948). The last two were uncompleted. Deren was born in Russia in 1917, and emigrated to the United States in 1922, with secondary school training at the League of Nations School in Geneva. She attended both Syracuse University and New York University, wrote poetry, developed an interest in the dance, and married a film maker. Deren, who died in 1961, was a socialist. She was a panel member of the now-famous symposium, "Poetry and the Film," which took place in New York City on October 28, 1953. Film critic Parker Tyler was also a panel member, as were playwright Arthur Miller and poet Dylan Thomas. Deren spoke for a personal, "vertical," poetic film against the jovial jibes of Dylan Thomas. For Deren, as she explained it on this panel and elsewhere, the poetic film centers around certain images and emotions, much like a dream does, rather than a "horizontal," more logical and linear development. The theoretical writings of Deren are developed particularly in *An Anagram of Ideas on Art, Form, and Film* (1946), and in "Cinematography: The Creative Use of Reality" (*Daedalus*, winter 1960). *An Anagram*, which has been published as an issue of *Film Culture* (no. 39), is composed of short essays, aphoristic statements, charts, and diagrams (party invitations too), and also reprints Deren's guest column for the *Village Voice* in which she sat in for Jonas Mekas in the summer of 1961. One pattern that emerges is that of a film maker bringing her thoughts about the cinema into line with her films: the hope, too, is to underscore the use of myth, dream, and symbol—in nonlinear or "irrational" aspect—by the use and placement of certain images rather than a standard narrative. Like poet H.D., Deren was consciously developing a feminist or matriarchal mythology with a creative mix of classical, astrological, and anthropological figures. Two important essays are "Notes, Essays, Letters," in *Film Culture* (winter 1965) and "Cinema as an Art Form" collected in Lewis Jacobs's *Introduction to the Art of the Movies* (1960). In these two essays can be seen the origin of many precepts of the avant-garde film. In "Notes, Essays, Letters," Deren advances the notion that her film *Meshes in the Afternoon* "is concerned with the interior experiences of an individual," with an emphasis on the subconscious interpretation, and symbolic value, of certain objects and situations. And in "Cinema as an Art Form," Deren makes an extremely important statement about the nature of the cinematic form: it is a "time-space art with a unique capacity for creating new temporal-spatial relationships." Not coincidentally, it emerges in an era when the radio, the airplane, the "rocket-ship" and the "theory of relativity in physics" all appear, and of course it is tied in with our perception of the twentieth century as an anarchic period. The deliberately unexplained "mixing" of time and space in the cinema, one deduces from her reasoning, is a perfect analogue for technological advances that cut across space and time, and that for Deren connect with nonlinear thought.

Deren criticizes Hollywood films in "Cinema as an Art Form," in an observation that will later be repeated by Michelson, for the loss of individual integrity and individual vision. But then much of this is traceable to the fact that although the camera is in reality quite "utilitarian," in Hollywood "let no one be guilty of achieving something with less expense, less fanfare and less trouble than can possibly be employed, for in that glittering system of values economy of any kind constitutes a debasement." Deren here decides that in mass film the faithful representation of reality is the important thing and that this is a factor in encouraging technical expertise. Though some of this is modified in her guest column for the *Village Voice* that concludes that compared to the cynicism of the French New Wave (particularly cynical is the use of the bomb in *Hiroshima Mon Amour*) the American film industry is full of innocent barbarians (August 25, 1960).

There are many similarities in the perceptions of Sontag, Michelson, and Deren about the poetic, self-contained, autonomous vision on which the avant-garde film depends. In her piece, "Toward Snow, Part One" in the June 1971 *Artforum,* for instance, Michelson gives a brilliant definition of the avant-garde film, tying in historical-cultural movements:

> The entire tradition of the independently made film, from Deren and Anger through Brakhage, had been developed as an extension, in American terms, of an avant-gardist position of the twenties in Europe, distending the continuity, negating the tension of narrative. Grounded in the experience of Surrealism and of Expressionism, its will to destroy narrative was an attempt to situate film in a kind of perpetual Present, one image or sequence succeeding another in rapid disjunction, tending, ultimately in furious pace of single-frame construction, to devour or eliminate expectation as a dimension of cinematic experience.

A writer most thorough in analyzing the Hollywood system is Hortense Powdermaker, author of *Hollywood: The Dream Factory,* which systematically and objectively dissects the Hollywood system. Powdermaker, who lived from 1900 to 1973, was a widely respected anthropologist who spent most of her adult life as a professor at Queens College in New York City. The inspiration to study Hollywood came when Powdermaker was living in Mississippi while doing research and noticed that the main form of entertainment available was movies. She extrapolated from this the extraordinary influence that film must have on American society. After *Hollywood: The Dream Factory* was published in 1950, however, Powdermaker never wrote about films or Hollywood again, claiming that while she respected that world she had no desire to become a part of it. Of course it is a curious, ironic twist that it is perhaps for this work that Powdermaker is now the most well-known. And for the present-day reader, the importance of *Hollywood: The Dream Factory* is that it is a completely objective view of the movie colony, neither from an insider's point of view nor—as seems more frequent among intellectuals—from the vantage point of someone with a bias against Hollywood. The book's introduction explains that during her year in California, working under the hypothesis that the "social system in which they [movies] are made significantly influences their contents and meaning," Powdermaker's objectivity was maintained because she "took the inhabitants in Hollywood and in the South Seas seriously, and this was pleasing to both," for to her "the handsome stars with their swimming-pool homes were no more glamorous than were the South Sea aborigines exotic."

The assumptions that underlie Powdermaker's study may seem Jungian or McLuhanesque, as she discovers similarities among advertising, radio, and movies as all being forces that "manipulate emotions and values," and that depend on the "mass production of dreams." She pinpoints many standard plot conventions and formulas (in fact, she seems to be the first, in 1950, to use that phrase or define the concept). And she sees that mankind in films, "according to Hollywood is either completely good, or bad," with a static personality showing little development either in "growth or regression."

Powdermaker observes that it is the "men who play God"—the executives and producers—who "have the greatest power to stamp the movies with their personal daydreams and fantasies." She properly pinpoints the fact that the producer controls not just the story or the script content, but also casting and cutting (as she refers to editing). The anthropologist cleverly uses the analogies at her fingertips, claiming that "as the Melanesians think failure would result from changing the form of a spell, so men in Hollywood consider it dangerous to depart from their formulas. Each group can point to the times it worked and conveniently forget or rationalize the other occasions. If the Melanesian uses taboos to placate 'hostile supernatural forces,' Hollywood appeases critics and enemies with the Motion Picture Association Code. Primitive men make sacrifices to court the supernatural . . . in Hollywood money is sacrificed in huge amounts." Here Deren's insight about the compulsion to spend money is underscored.

Chapters are devoted to the screenwriters and the directors, with "real-life" examples described, although Powdermaker uses clever pseudonyms like "Mr. Hopeful," "Mr. Pretentious," "Mr. Cynic," or "Miss Sanguine." Her objectivity allows her to debunk the old myth of the casting couch: in the chapter on "Stars," the anthropologist observes that some actresses sleep with people to get a first break, but Powdermaker concludes that the successful ones would probably have made it anyway. The same conclusion is drawn about young men who escort important women, or male homosexuals who play up to important men executives.

Of course all Powdermaker's observations are based on a 1940s studio system, in which the "primacy of the director" had not yet taken hold. And surely the cinema has since that time come up with some heroes and heroines more complicated in emotional structure than those Powdermaker describes. But her observations about their impact still hold; they are "heroes and heroines of modern society and bear some resemblance to the heroes of primitive and preindustrial societies which also had cycles of stories revolving, and highly stylized characters." Moreover, the relationship of "fans to their stars is not limited to seeing them in movies, any more than primitive people's relationship to their totemic heroes is limited to hearing a myth told occasionally." For while in the early-1980s we no longer have the same number of "fan magazines" Powdermaker is referring to, there are a variety of other publications available for purchase in supermarkets and drug stores that see film stars as pop figures about whom we are privy to private information which is easy to discern as puffed up, or just false. Even so, the mythic aura is maintained.

One other critic who quite successfully discusses what a "star" quality is as opposed to a simply very good mimetic, or acting ability, is French critic Claude-Edmonde Magny, author of *The Age of the American Novel: The Film Aesthetic of Fiction Between the Two Wars,* and other books, including *The History of the French Novel Since 1918.* Magny, who was born in 1913 and died in 1966, was the first woman to be admitted to the Ecole Normale Supérieur. With a degree in philosophy, she held a number of posts at various French universities, and at Cambridge University and Princeton University. When it was published in 1948, *The Age of the American Novel* created a critical stir in France, but it was not translated into English until the early-1970s. Magny concentrates on the influence of the film on novelists such as Hemingway, Dos Passos, Steinbeck, and Faulkner, but also points out the importance of the director as the auteur, or author of the film. Like other European woman critics, Magny was able to see—as early as the 1940s—that the director of a film would assume primary importance and that eventually libraries would own entire collections of a director's work.

Like Powdermaker and the earlier C.A. Lejeune Magny sees that some stars, such as Katharine Hepburn (with her "prominent cheekbones, vibrant personality, and Bryn Mawr accent") or Joan Crawford (who has an "overlarge mouth and heavy jaw") can transcend or combine with the roles they play. Garbo and Dietrich are others, like Chaplin, who manage to create a "collective consensus." Magny draws a parallel to fiction; we may see the same "star-like" qualities in the "heroines of great novels." What is notable about Magny's work is that it presents in scholarly format what might be otherwise regarded as superficial or light observations. A sharp comparison can be made, for instance, with André Bazin's description of Charlie Chaplin in *What Is Cinema?* For as focused on Chaplin's individual features as he is, Bazin doesn't make the extraordinary cultural tie-ins, or even the across-role generalities. Just so, Roland Barthes's brief essay on "The Face of Garbo" focuses on certain of her features, "the curve of the nostrils," "the arch of the eyebrows," yet these details express an "existential from an essential beauty." Her myth stands for Woman, rather than a culturally symbolic essential Garbo.

Much of Magny's generalizations depend upon her perception of the film and the novel as having mass origins. The cinema in particular is an "art of the masses, the entertainment of those without leisure." Like Powdermaker, Magny reminds us of economic realities of films: to be profitable they must be viewed by large numbers of people. And in common with many theoreticians (Sontag among them) when they first begin to analyze the effects of the cinema, Magny's introduction contains a fine comparision between the theatre and the cinema. Among critics comparing film and the theatre, she is the first, in 1948, to discuss the very private condition of film: going into the "two arms of our seat" as opposed to the very public nature of theatre group. She concludes that "it is incomparably easier to maintain one's freedom of judgment in a movie house than in a playhouse." And Magny emphasizes here the narrative qualities of the cinema in contrast to the "spectacle-like" stage. The new temporal arrangement, or the simultaneity of cinema, is mentioned as well, plus the possibility that "the movies, generally considered an instrument that dulls the perception, may actually re-educate the perception and intelligence of the spectator by accustoming him to understanding things without long observation."

Shared themes and insights are to be found in the works comparing novel, theatre, and film by Sontag and Magny although Magny's obviously predates Sontag's by nearly 20 years. Magny concentrates on the influence of cinematic techniques—ellipsis, parallel editing, and so on—resulting in rapid prose movement and projective reporting, while Sontag is more concerned with setting aesthetic boundaries, and in discussing the interseeding of the arts. Magny calls it cross-fertilization, Sontag terms its purest form synaesthesia.

Magny and Powdermaker—one a "foreigner" to the American cinematic scene and the other an "objective" outside observer-anthropologist—each stress the mass origins of the cinema, particularly the American film, although Magny, as a critic with a literary bent, sees the film as the product of one vision, or auteur. And of course so do the critics who are writing postauteur theory popularization: Sontag and Michelson, each of whom are more than partisan in expressing their admiration for various directors. While it's fun to observe that Michelson, in her highbrow fashion, makes a somewhat snide reference to the auteur theory as being one that was "an endorsement of narrative conventions in cinema that was to produce the orthodoxy of the sixties and its attendant strategy, 'la politique des auteurs'" ("Screen/Surface: The Politics of Illusion," *Artforum,* September 1972). And, even more snobbishly, she has called the American awareness and acceptance of the auteur theory "belated."

Michelson and Deren are openly critical of Hollywood; Sontag only implicitly so in her support of non-mainstream work. All three militate for the avant-garde or cult film, while only Michelson and Sontag see the subversive possibilities in film. The women film critics discussed here have sounded widely different aesthetic boundaries as well. While Magny and Powdermaker describe the mass origins of art, and Sontag underscores this approach by a leftist or Marxist orientation, others, like Deren or Michelson, limn the formal, contained, "poetic" moment or image of a film. Which of course does not keep either of them from seeing a film—not to be taken as an expression of a "grassroots" consciousness—that opposes the concept of "Hollywood." And for Michelson it *should* function in a subversive way, even if it's the expression of an isolated or elitist sensibility. Just so, the sensuous surface of film art for Sontag is to be lovingly admired, although she still discusses the aesthetic, philosophical, and social significance of a film. Even within just these five critical approaches, many of the major theoretical stances can be observed: mythic, sociological, Marxist, poetic or avant garde. In addition, we can also see some of the particular predilections of women film critics: the openness to the interseeding of the cinema with other arts, especially as emphasized by Michelson and Sontag, and a true awareness of audience response, particularly the effect of "stars" and their "micro-physiognomy" on the audience.

6

Iris Barry:

Historian and All-Round Critic

Undoubtedly the most dynamic woman in the history of film scholarship was Iris Barry (1895–1969), film critic, historian, and the first film curator of the Museum of Modern Art. British-born Barry was very nearly the first woman film critic in England; she wrote for *The Spectator* from 1923 to 1930 (as we have seen, fellow Briton C.A. Lejeune started to review in 1922), and was film editor of *The Daily Mail* from 1926 to 1930. In 1926 Barry published her very popular *Let's Go to the Pictures* (later retitled *Let's Go to the Movies*) and after her move to the United States, wrote a book on the significance of the pioneer film maker, *D.W. Griffith, American Film Master* (1940). Even discounting her reviews and earlier book and film curatorial work for the Museum of Modern Art, to have popularized the work of Griffith and explained it in so comprehensive a fashion—with stills, analysis, and filmography—is a feat so extraordinary as to mark a prominent place for Barry in the world of film scholarship.

In the United States, Barry was also a regular book reviewer for the New York *Herald Tribune,* and her articles appeared in various popular American magazines. With seemingly boundless energy, she gave courses in cinema studies while working at the Museum of Modern Art, wrote program notes as well as the First Bulletin of the Film Library. Some would say that her work as a curator was the most significant, as she cadged films and books, hustled grant money, and essentially created the entire film archive. She also compiled and edited *The Film Index*—a long volume treating all aspects of film—for the WPA Writers' Project of the Roosevelt era, and during World War II worked to get political refugees out of Europe. Somehow, she managed to squeeze in translations, biographies, and novels, too.

Consistently pioneering and enterprisingly partisan, Barry was attracted to the cinema as a young woman at a time when the film was much less than respectable. During World War I she held down a number of unconventional jobs, for example, shipping telephone poles and ordering guns, employment highly unlikely at that time for a woman. Shortly after the war Barry became a film critic. She helped found the London Film Society and—according to Alistair Cooke—left England after being fired from *The Daily Mail* for demanding too much money and a trip to Hollywood. Cooke quotes Barry as saying she was "severed rather forcefully" (*New York Times,* January 18, 1970). Yet another version, in Russell Lynes's *Good Old Modern,* is that she was fired after submitting a negative review of a Marion Davies film. (Actress Davies was the paramour of publisher William Randolph Hearst.)

Some reports say that Barry was alone when she came to New York, others that she was already married to John Abbot, a Wall Street banker and executive vice president of the Museum of Modern Art. Barry seems to have kept some veils around her private life, although her flamboyant writing style was matched by her personal life; at one point she and Abbot were working together, though maritally separated. Alfred Barr, the first director of the Museum of Modern Art, "remembered" that she had been a founding member of the London Film Society and set her to "doing something about a film collection." John Hay Whitney gave money for a preliminary study of how to set up a film collection. With a grant from the Rockefeller Foundation, Barry went to Hollywood for a year to determine the intricacies of such a set-up, and also to get films from Hollywood's stockpile. This was the origin of the MOMA's Art Film Library, now called the Film Department.

Yet Barry's reputation might be established by her criticism alone. Barry's first book, *Let's Go to the Movies,* which was published in 1926 when she was turning 31, was a major success in both the United States and England. In it one can find many pronouncements about the aesthetic and psychological nature of the cinema. To some this may come as a surprise, for it is easy to let Barry's at times slangy style get in the way of some very fine observations, made even more significant because of their pioneer nature. Comparing the theatre and the cinema, an early exercise, as we have seen, for most major cinematic critics in the beginning stages of their careers, Barry speaks of the logistically easy approach to the cinema as compared to going to the drama, which entails ticket buying, planning ahead, and so on. She also likens the cinema to the dream state as many others have: "we come out of the pictures soothed and drugged like sleepers wakened, having half-forgotten our own existence, hardly knowing our own names. The theatre is a tonic, the cinema a sedative. The cinema is a liberation of the ego, the theatre an enrichment of it. And that is why, after the feverish activity of a day of modern life, the screen calls to us more strongly than the footlights."

It is this respite from agitation, Barry says, that makes the cinema so attractive, not just the fact that it is "cheap, accessible, a popular not a social entertainment." Nor—and here she's at her sprightly best—do you "have to put your best clothes on to see Harold Lloyd fall off a sky-scraper."

Barry annotates the bias against the cinema in England in the 1920s, particularly among the professional classes. She also analyzes the fact that the critic of the drama—or the Dramatic Critic as she denominates him/her—is much more well thought of than the critic of the cinema.

And she makes some rather respectable conjectures about the reasons for the popularity of the cinema. It is because, she declares, the religious impulse has died out, with its attendant ecstasy and despair. Like "other drugs," going to movies is also a habit. And she makes note of the popular origins of cinematic art form. It owes its birth to the "livelier, more democratic side" of the theatre. Too, it often gets blamed—much like the "novelettes" used to be—for the ills of society. In the chapter "Stars," Barry observes that probably the illusion of "intimacy with film stars" accounts for part of the film's success, and in fact the personalizing effects of stars on critics and audiences has been an assumption of most present-day criticism.[1]

Like other European critics, Barry is very good at defining the qualities of various national cinemas, and also at cleverly discussing different directors, such as Lubitsch, von Sternberg, and de Mille. Even though Hitchcock is only just on the scene, Barry spots him as a "promising recruit for the future." In general, she seems to be in favor of the narrative film and not particularly disposed to avant-garde art, as we might expect from a critic who stresses the "democratic" origins of film.

Barry, interestingly, predicts the coming importance of the Russian film. And particularly in her discussion of individual directors we may observe Barry's quite clever style. Von Sternberg "came up like the Evening Star and went down like a meteor." Though she is not, Barry proclaims, "an admirer of Mr. Cecil B. de Mille," she admits that "he has a perfect genius for vulgarity in every sense of the word." Her example: "*The Ten Commandments* is his wash-pot, and over Reincarnation he has cast out his shoe. I shall never feel the same either about the decalogue or about reincarnation now that I have seen what Mr. de Mille has done with them."

Critically prescient, this early book draws together many important critical threads later made much of when made into the gowns of high criticism. A chatty tone that unfortunately dated to quaintness more quickly than Lejeune's or Bryher's contemporaneous books camouflaged both auteurist and sociological approaches to the cinema, as well as a good awareness of the working of the industry: Particularly pertinent in light of Barry's later career is what she calls the "cinema's mutability." Of course what she is referring to is the evanescence of the actual films, not the cinema's aesthetic character (a condition that she devoted much of the rest of her life to changing). Barry complains: "A film appears, say in the Charing Cross Road, for three days. One hears about it a day too late. Where can one look for it? There is no means of knowing. Those who know the ropes can, of course, by discovering the name of the company that owns it, ring them up and find out where it is to be seen. But the public doesn't know that trick, and in any case why should it?" The availability, the permanence, of films is a "problem" Barry discusses in her chapter "Difficulties" (quotes above from *Let's Go to the Movies*).

And she also takes a stab at a theory about women and film. In 1926, this is an early, and admittedly primitive, effort. In trying to determine how screenplays could be improved, she decides that the writers should be women rather than men because women are more visual, and because the cinema is more for women than men. In this chapter, "Difficulties," she does not give specific support for her observations, but in a later chapter "The Public's Pleasure," she analyzes the appeal of the cinema for women, and is more sardonic than any present-day feminist in criticizing the content of such films. Because "three out of every four of all cinema audiences are women," films have been designed to please women with their "over-whelming, apparently meaningless, and immensely conventional love interests." About which Barry observes that the "insistence on marriage, or conjunction of male and female, as the end of difficulties is of course due to the fact that in actual experience we find it the beginning of difficulties." Moreover, in answer to the rhetorical question *"Do* women usually marry the first young man they meet under suitable circumstances? No, they don't, and they tend to do so less every year." For this popular mythology, Barry blames the "printing press," the novels and plays that have popularized this notion. Like C.A. Lejeune she asserts that both "the printing press and the film fantasy" present people with "false dreams for fear they kick at true facts." For the cinema doesn't present sociological facts and since, according to Barry, the cinema must "develop or die," she recommends that women write to film producers and demand more realistic stories.

Of course from the point of view of film scholarship or film history, the most significant achievement of Barry's—most probably of any film critic at that time—is her work on Griffith. Although *D.W. Griffith: American Film Master* went out of print soon after its publication in 1940, it has since been reissued. Barry was among the first to recognize the importance of Griffith, and the book contains a major section that shows her acknowledgment of the technical innovations Griffith made. She sees that, despite his stage training, he managed to perceive that a camera could and should be moved in the middle of a scene. With the help of his cameraman, G.W. "Billy" Bitzer, the very striking effects of light and shade are implemented, particularly in *Edgar Allan Poe,* or in the scene using firelight in *A Drunkard's Reformation* (both 1909). Griffith picked up on and enlarged Porter's cross-cutting technique in the 1903 *The Great Train Robbery;* in *The Lonely Villa* (1909) and *The Lonedale Operator* (1911) Griffith perfects this technique to accommodate the last-minute rescue. In heightening the emotional intensity of the cinema, Griffith thereby increased the possibilities for scene tinting. Yet another innovation of Griffith's—as odd as it may now seem to cite this—was increased length for the cinema (here Barry forgets or ignores early, long films by the British and Italians). This book alone, with its clear and detailed understanding of the significance of D.W. Griffith, marks Barry as a major critic and film historian (especially when one considers that Eisenstein's very much acclaimed work on Griffith appeared in 1942, two years later than Barry's Griffith book, and that a comprehensive overview of Griffith helped established the critical reputation of film historian Louis Jacobs, although unlike Barry's book, *The Rise of the American Film* has been in constant use).

Barry was made film curator of the Museum of Modern Art in 1935, and became its director in 1947 (while working as a curator, Barry taught a course at Columbia University, "The History, Aesthetic and Technique of the Motion Picture"). Because Griffith, according to present-day film curator Eileen Bowser, found it difficult in the 1930s to pay storage bills, he allowed the Museum to acquire his films and his collection of correspondence and documents. And during the 1930s Barry also obtained the work of a number of European "avant-garde" artists as well, including Man Ray, Marcel Duchamp, René Clair, and Germaine Dulac. Film, as she and her staff defined it for their permanent collections, ranged from an "experimental" film like Leger's 1928 *Ballet Mécanique* to a more "popular" classic like Porter's *The Great Train Robbery.*

Barry was publishing articles in many popular magazines, while working at the Modern and writing the first Program Notes and Bulletin of the Film Library.[2] Even though she was writing expository pieces on various directors such as Pabst, Lubitsch, Porter, and von Stroheim, Barry's clever style still comes through. In writing about Lubitsch's *The Love Parade* (1929) for instance, she can discuss its importance as a technical advancement—visually and aurally—while still slyly noting "the surprising manner in which the royal heroine bursts into song without apparent provocation."

Pieces that trace the "Post-War [WW I] American Films," as well as the importance of European film makers, also see films as genre, like the "gangster film," and the mythological and sociological interpretation of the "good-bad-man," along with the romanticization of contemporary critical figures.[3] Seeing films, in 1935, as genre, myth, and sociology was light years beyond contemporaneous cinema criticism.

And always, Barry is cognizant and proud of the middlebrow or populist aspects of film. In a piece for *Vogue,* she reviews *Stella Dallas* (1925) and declares that "for the first time a film which is a melodrama pure and simple, can claim the distinction of being thoroughly well-played throughout. . . . *Stella Dallas* is one of the simplest, one of the best constructed and certainly the best-acted of films of a popular kind which has ever come out of a studio. The fact that it is above no one's head is a merit." Her predilections can be observed in an essay as important as the preface to Lewis Jacobs's *The Rise of the American Film* where Barry asserts: "Perhaps the idea that art is something particular and for the few has to be further dispelled before we can approach the film honestly, for there has been some shame about its immense popularity." Besides, the rise of the commercial film is "really a romance. It is the colorful tale of as typical a group of Americans as one could hope to hear of."

Barry is as committed to promoting the documentary film, and its "great capacity for fact, for unveiling in its own peculiarly veracious way the whole fact of life [which] has been relatively neglected" (New York *Times,* January 6, 1943). And though war may have changed some of this, according to Barry, we need this instrument in peacetime too to help the man in the street "grasp the complexities of the world." After a query as to who the sponsors of such documentary films may be (the government up until then had funded most), Barry explains the work of the Museum of Modern Art in this regard. She also uses this article to catalogue and underscore the importance of documentary film makers Robert Flaherty (*Nanook of the North,* 1921), John Grierson (*Night Mail,* 1936), and Pare Lorenz (*The River,* 1938) among others. Barry can declare prophetically that some day "film scholars" will "turn earnestly to films, such as *The* [sic] *Triumph of the Will,* made in a very different vein by the Nazis themselves to delude their own people." It is, Barry says, a pleasing thought that out of their own documentation the "Nazi chieftains are today being indicted in Nuremburg: film is a legal document, too."

With a less serious style but with the same intent Barry makes a number of the same points in an October 1946 *Town and Country* article, "The Film of Fact," and in a July 1943 *Home and Food* piece entitled "Films and Reality." As partisan as she is about the newsreel reportage of World War II, she is just as messianic about the salvation of certain films. Some of her work on the preservation of film is quite cleverly explained in article "Why Wait for Posterity?" which appears in the January 1946 *Hollywood Quarterly.* "Since the cobbler's children are always the worst shod," Barry cheekily begins her piece, it is natural that Hollywood might be the last place where past films are taken seriously. And though it is true, Barry notes, that certain film executives occasionally speak about preserving films for posterity, "in the spirit, presumably, of those who seal up cans of Spam, phonograph records, and newspapers in the foundations of new buildings," very little had actually been done to make it possible to literally see the screen classics of the past. The remainder of Barry's piece gives a history of the film collection—not only the obtaining of prints but also the important matter of funding—and speaks about similar screening programs at other museums and universities.

Iris Barry seemed to never lack for a new venue by which to popularize, publicize, and sometimes to polemicize film, whether as reviewer, curator, or historian. And while she was not able to conduct all her activities simultaneously throughout her life, there is no woman film critic who had a comparable group or listing. She also saw the cinema in many new theoretical fashions: nationally, auteuristically, sociologically, and as genre and myth. Barry has early insights into film's analogies with the dream state, and a primitive stab at some ideas about women and film. Her urgency about film preservation and the unearthing of D.W. Griffiths' work may have been that for which she is most well known to date, but there is no question that her other work demands as much attention. Despite an occasional tendency to flipness, Iris Barry may be the most versatile critic of either sex to address the cinema.

NOTES

1. For a discussion of "intimacy" from the point of view of television aesthetics, see Horace Newcomb, *T.V.: The Most Popular Art* (New York: Anchor Press, 1975).

2. In interesting contrast, the current curator of the MOMA Film Department has said that she prefers to "take the long view" and be a historian rather than critic, for "in sitting down and writing what I thought of something I might change my mind" (an interview with Bowser in New York City, July 1978). Still, Bowser—who catalogued the Griffith collection—has updated Barry's work on Griffith in *D.W. Griffith: American Film Master* (1965) and written a number of film articles as well as *Film Notes* for the Museum of Modern Art. Finding lost or damaged films is what pleases her most: "Romantic that I am, I believe that somewhere, in somebody's attic or barn, in some former distribution office in Illinois or Peking, the great films still exist" ("'Lost' Films are Found in the Most Unexpected Places," *New York Times*, June 25, 1978).

3. The phrase the "good-bad girl" is used by Nathan Leites and Martha Wolfenstein in *Movies: A Psychological Study* (New York: Atheneum, 1970), one of the very few books to see film psychoanalytically. Also see Hugo Munsterberg, *The Film: A Psychological Study* (New York: Dover, 1969).

7

The Culture Critics:

Diana Trilling, Simone de Beauvoir,
Joan Didion, and Nora Sayre

If one thinks it is still to be proven that women film critics generally react more directly, more intimately—and in some cases more
imaginatively—to the performer in films under their scrutiny than male
critics, the responses of women writers as intellectually formidable as
Simone de Beauvoir and Diana Trilling should settle the question. In
fact, no one seems as surprised to encounter such subjective and intense
reactions as Trilling herself, in partial apology for her "late" apprecia-
tion of the star, in the 1963 essay "The Death of Marilyn Monroe."
While the essay surely can be seen in the light of the women's movement's posthumous canonization of Monroe, it is more than latter-day
feminist guilt purgation. Trilling's article is an extraordinary example of
the free interplay of autobiographical intrusions from the writer, nearly
"cinematic" projections onto/into the actor's psyche, and cultural generalizations.

The writer's reaction to, sometimes fantasized interaction with,
the actor-actress is often taken to be paradigmatic of the culture, and for
these purposes, biographical details, even gossip, about the personal life
of the star are freely mixed in. At first, easy, glance it would seen as if
the work of Norman Mailer on Marilyn Monroe would perfectly fit this
description. But his 1973 biography, *Marilyn,* is a clear demonstration of
an only superficial attempt—though of course not necessarily a conscious one—at this method. He may buy, he reports to us, in the true
vicarious modus operandi of the new journalist, a bottle of Chanel No. 5
(Monroe was "famous for having worn it"), but he would never "have a
real clue to how it smelled on her skin." The biographical details are
meticulously recorded, as are show biz minutiae about each of her films,
but nowhere does there emerge the creative conjunction one might expect from the chief autobiographical and impressionistic journalist of

our age. The portrait's ultimate flatness makes a telling comparison with Trilling's essay, or with a piece like Simone de Beauvoir's brilliant if sporadically connective essay on Brigitte Bardot, "Brigitte Bardot and the Lolita Syndrome."

For in these pieces—as in others by culture critics Joan Didion and Nora Sayre that also consider the cumulative work of an actor, or of the ellision between actor and role—the distance, in the words of Beauvoir, between "Mr. Chaplin and Charlie is entirely done away with"; it is an "ambiguous presence—that both of the actor and of the character he is playing." (These remarks are preparatory to her discussion of *Modern Times*, and also to her comments on more contemporary films such as *Bonnie and Clyde, Five Easy Pieces,* and the films of James Bond and Clint Eastwood [Beauvoir assiduously avoids the French farce, she reports]. These observations are found in the fourth volume of her autobiography, *All Said and Done*.) Even the fact that Beauvoir knows "Yves Montand's face too well" doesn't prevent her from seeing him as Lambrakis in *Z;* "soon the actor and the character merged into one."

This acceptance of the amalgam is put into automatic practice in the work of Trilling on Marilyn Monroe. Trilling has been the fiction critic of *The Nation;* essayist and reviewer in the *New York Times,* and *Partisan Review,* among other places; and author of *Claremont Essays, We Must March My Darlings, Reviewing the Forties,* and the recent reportorial *Mrs. Harris.* Born in New York City in 1905, daughter of a successful businessman, she married renowned literary critic and Columbia University professor Lionel Trilling, and they had one child, a son. Diana Trilling—a momentous figure herself—determined never to teach, she is reported to have said in conversation, after having once taken over a class of her husband's and deciding that it jangled her nerves too much.

Trilling's essay on Monroe is, quite simply, a surprise. For one thing, the combination of psychobiography and high-level movie magazine reportage is a new one for this kind of writer, and for criticism in general. By brilliant conjecture, Trilling makes the kind of intuitive leap Mailer's piece tries for but fails at; her "feeling about Marilyn Monroe" is that "even when she had spoken of 'wanting to die' she really meant she wanted to end her suffering, not her life." Or, in noting Monroe's incredibly upbeat qualities, "when there is this much need for optimism surely there is great peril, and the public got the message."

Coming from another type of writer some of these insights might be regarded as platitudinous; as we also might dismiss as gossipy a report that a few of the men Trilling knew who had had "romantic" involvments with Monroe found her sweet and lovable, though not particularly sexual. But when it is Trilling who concludes that "Monroe's perception of herself came from others' reactions to her," that her biolog-

ical "gift" did not arise from any sure self-knowledge, we are more inclined to accept the summation. Trilling has earlier on put herself in a
"special" category vis a vis Monroe criticism: there is "always this
shield of irony some of us raise between ourselves and any object of
popular adulation, and I had made my dull point of snubbing her pictures."

But she's changed her mind after watching a "television trailer of
Bus Stop." The junction of high and low culture (and our disinclination
to question the hybrid) is—since the advent of new journalism—a hallmark of the confident intellect. But where Mailer, especially in *Marilyn,*
fails to come up with the flashy insight that *should* result from the unexpected juxtaposition, both Trilling and Beauvoir have startling success.
When Trilling has her conversion about Monroe, it's because "an illumination, a glow of something beyond the ordinarily human" had gone on
in the room. Illumination is a cleverly used television adjective that
moves rapidly into a psychoanalytic interpretation probably borrowed
from literary criticism. It is a natural for psychobiographical cinema
criticism that might be seen to have taken its most primitive form in
early issues of *Photoplay* and *Modern Screen.* For Trilling, Monroe's
luminosity comes from her innocence, from being untouched by life (a
quality shared, according to Trilling, with Hemingway). And finally—
here is the tie-in with her suicide—from being able to "suffer one's experience without being able to learn self-protection."

It is as disarming, as refreshing, to find Beauvoir starting her long
separately published essay on Bardot, "Brigitte Bardot and the Lolita
Syndrome," also in reaction to a television appearance—Bardot's on
New Year's Eve. "Once again," Beauvoir says, "I could observe that
Brigitte Bardot was disliked in her own country." If Beauvoir's style
here seems more fluid, more natural, than in some of her other work, it's
perhaps because a historical or critical apparatus has been dropped, for
the subject apparently demands less of a pronouncement, less of a commitment to posterity. Daughter—like Trilling—of a bourgeois family
(her father was an advocate in the Court of Appeals in Paris), Beauvoir
was born in 1908. University professor, essayist, social historian, and
novelist, her work includes the novels *The Mandarins* and *L'Invitée,* her
multivolumed autobiography, *All Said and Done,* and the monumental
The Second Sex, the last inspired by the suggestion of her life-time in-
amorato and intellectual companion, Jean-Paul Sartre, that she "look
into" the fact that she wasn't "brought up the same way a boy would
have been." This model for the twentieth-century intellectual woman
has no difficulty seeing the cinema as important material for analysis

(even including the textually integrated reviews in *All Said and Done*).

As a member of the TV audience, Beauvoir dissents from her countrymen's antipathy toward Bardot, which tells the observing critic that the bohemian star appeals more to freedom-loving Americans than to the middle-class French, who feel threatened by her. For Bardot—a Lolita-like, youthful sex-object who makes use of the fact that "distancing creates erotic desire"—undermines a bourgeois structure (according to Beauvoir, the feminist historian, when one myth is threatened, so are all others).

In this regard and others, Beauvoir's version of Bardot is that she takes an active part in the construction of her persona. This has been a conscious, shared effort by both Bardot and (then) director-husband-mentor Roger Vadim. Not just actor-as-auteur, or merge of person and part, but conscious manipulator of the media, and of the national psyche. It is an intriguing cross-fertilization, as Beauvoir sees it. "In so far as she [Bardot] is exposed to the public gaze, her legend has been fed by her private life no less than by her film roles." (If so, it is a more sophisticated manipulation of 1950s mores than Monroe's.) While Monroe, according to Trilling, liberated Americans by making sexuality seem not so threatening (her childish "innocence" is the vehicle), Beauvoir decides that French men find Bardot particularly threatening because her "eroticism is not magical, but aggressive. The male is an object to her, just as she is to him. And that is precisely what wounds masculine pride."

Besides, like Lolita, Bardot has "not been marked by experience." Her hairdo is that of a waif; seen from behind she is "almost androgynous." She goes about "barefooted, she turns up her nose at elegant clothes, jewels, girdles, perfumes, make-up, at all artifice," "Radical innocence" here is not the star's undoing as it is for an American critic like Trilling. Perhaps only Americans see the tragic potentiality in innocence, lost or otherwise. (That they are untouched, however, is an almost common observation about women stars; a May 3, 1981 *New York Times* essay on Elizabeth Taylor's first stage appearance, in *The Little Foxes,* for instance, notes her curiously innocent and untouched quality even after six marriages, various and numerous tribulations, and so forth.)

The attention to physical detail, followed by social or psycho-cultural generalizations, seems an irresistible venue for women writers. This is not simply an example of woman's proverbial obsession with physical assets, as a quick sidelook at Alexander Walker's otherwise quite effective description of Elizabeth Taylor in *The Celluloid Sacrifice* shows: Her "large eyes, delicate nose and dark hair that always looks more effective when let down" is the kind that an "Elizabethan poet would have called 'gipsy.'" But—unlike Beauvoir or others such as

Sayre who move these descriptions into other realms—Walker simply cites the cultural stereotype and lets it go at that; Taylor's looks hold "sexual tension," and "generate expectancy among filmgoers that her actions will be impulsive, high-tempered, possibly destructive." As far as Mailer gets with this sort of thing is to say that Monroe seems to take on the characteristics of the man she is involved with (viz her physical agility in the dance sequences of *Gentlemen Prefer Blondes* when she is married to Joe DiMaggio), but he generally limits the attention to physical details to the usual reportage. He notes that before it was snipped, Monroe's formerly overlong nose appeared "snout-like," her teeth before correction were too protruding, causing her to tremulously quiver her upper lip, a retained habit.

Most telling, after reading Beauvoir's treatment of Bardot, is Parker Tyler's vision of the same star in *Sex, Psyche, Etcetera in the Film.* For Tyler, Bardot, with "canonic plenitude up front, facile nudity and long, tumbling blonde hair, was an impressive paradox; a cheerful Magdalene. Repentance and guilt were alien to her if only because her assets (like Jane Russell's before her) were so unmistakably God-given." Of the physicality of Bardot, Beauvoir can make so much more: "nothing can be read into Bardot's face. It is what it is. It has the forthright presence of reality. It is a stumbling-block to lewd fantasies and ethereal dreams alike. Most Frenchmen like to indulge in mystic flights as a change from ribaldry, and vice-versa. With BB they get nowhere." It is easy of course, and often unfair, to juxtapose quotes to advantage or disadvantage. But it is an undeniable truth that these major women writers and intellectuals here evoke their material almost "from within," as may be possible with no other subject matter. Lest this sound anti-feminist in suggesting "woman's intuition," let Beauvoir's explanation stand: "Sometimes, when I discuss a film with friends—friends whose tastes are the same as mine in other fields—I find that my opinion is quite unlike theirs: the film has certainly touched them or me or all of us in some intimate, entirely personal area." And then she starts to analyze the aesthetic qualities of actors' faces (in *All Said and Done*).

Tracing through the cultural implications of an actor is a specialty of writer Joan Didion, as her essay "John Wayne: A Love Song," in *Slouching Towards Bethlehem*, demonstrates. Didion's discovery that Wayne has cancer sends her, and by extension, her generation, into a kind of existential panic: "It did not seem possible that such a man could fall ill, could carry within him that most inexplicable and ungovernable of diseases. The rumor struck some obscure anxiety, threw our very childhoods into question." Like Beauvoir and Trilling, Didion sees her reaction as nationally paradigmatic: by riding through her child-hood, and "perhaps through yours" Wayne altered forever the shape of "our dreams." The occasion of the essay in which Didion makes these comments is an assignment that takes her in 1965 to the set of the most "recent" Wayne film where she has dinner with the man whose "face across the table was in certain ways more familiar than my husband's." Not because she's ever met Wayne before, but because of the intensity of her dream or fantasy life about him. For, less prosaically, "Deep in that part of my heart where the artificial rain forever falls" there is still a line she is waiting to hear from John Wayne.

The presence of the star—real or imagined—seems more acute in essays written by women critics, as does their own presence in the midst of these celebrities. The writer is a cultural conductor, a seismograph of the most significant proportions, who determines—by virture of her own response— the star's possible impact on society. In Joan Didion's review-essay about Woody Allen's *Manhattan, Interiors,* and *Annie Hall,* for instance, her reactions to the films' characters are so extreme as to be in the realm of interaction or reminiscence: "The characters in these pictures are, at best trying," Didion observes in an August 17, 1979 piece in the *New York Review of Books.* "They are morose. They have bad manners. They seem to take long walks and go to smart res-taurants only to ask one another hard questions." The more banal dia-logue is quoted, ending with "finally, inevitably, 'what does your analyst say." Didion doesn't like these characters, for any number of reasons. They are New Yorkers, they are self-conscious, they are intellectual and introspective in a way that Didion—a Californian whose own elitism does not include the Upper West Side leftist-intellectual value system of Allen and his characters—clearly despises.

The interesting point here is that she is reacting to them *as if* they were real. And as if Allen-as-director were himself in the film (an easy trick, admittedly, with this film maker. Within the *NYRB* piece, Di-dion's focus shifts to an interview with Woody Allen, printed elsewhere, in which he talks about his own analysis, and then to Didion's declara-tion that such introspection, such "working on" oneself, is adolescent and self-indulgent.

An easy slide, since the essay, called of course "Letter from 'Man-hattan,'" begins with assertions that self-absorption is endemic to the summer of 1979, a summer loaded with affectations and vanities. In the "large coastal cities of the United States this summer," Didion ob-serves, "many people wanted to be dressed in 'real linen,' as well as wanting to be served the 'perfect vegetable terrine,'" and—but of course—bothered to stand in line to see Woody Allen's *Manhattan.* Di-dion's rhetorical habit of the clever listing and the startling juxtaposi-tion has already been smartly satirized in Barbara Grizutti Harrison's piece on Didion, "Only Disconnect," which caused quite a stir when it was first published in *The Nation* (October 1979, collected in *Off Center,* New York: Dial Press, 1980). One needs only to read a Burpee catalogue, Harrison says, or to put some disparate "items" like Al Capone and sweet williams in the same sentence. But Didion also uses—particularly in this *NYRB* essay—the downwardly spiraling listing, with the deflationary detail at the end (a technique not unfamiliar to readers of eighteenth-century satirical poetry). *Manhattan*'s Tracy, for instance, is characterized as having "perfect skin, perfect wisdom, perfect sex, and no visible family."

Here the culture critic as social chronicler can be seen in perfect operation. The telling, damning detail is discerned. In Didion's case, however, her moralizing is a surprise, even though the subject about which she most moralizes is life in New York City. So many of Didion's essays call up the fact that not only is she a "California girl," but that she's from an old Valley family (see especially "On Going Home" and "Notes From a Native Daughter" in *Slouching Towards Bethlehem*). "Hollywood the Destroyer" lurks somewhere "in the wilds between the Thalia and the Museum of Modern Art" Didion observes ironically in her essay that defends that fabled West Coast corrupter, "I Can't Get That Monster Out of My Mind."

Didion, born in 1935 and praised by the *New York Times* as the best prose writer of her generation, is novelist, *Run River, Play It As It Lays,* and *A Book of Common Prayer;* screenwriter, of *A Star is Born* and *True Confessions,* with her husband John Gregory Dunne; and essayist. The pieces in *Slouching Towards Bethlehem*—by now a classic collection—were originally written for magazines such as *Vogue,* the *New York Times Magazine,* and the *Saturday Evening Post.* For a time in the mid-1970s, Didion wrote a column about Hollywood, "The Coast," for *Esquire.* And in 1979, another collection of essays, *The White Album,* was published to reviews not quite as glowing as those received by *Slouching Towards Bethlehem.* To say her work is autobiographical is in some ways to miss the point, to undershoot the mark, since she has nearly made a literary cult of neurasthenic projection. And while it comes as no surprise to read her adoring portrait of John Wayne, or her condemnation of Woody Allen and his works, which is in many ways a profile, it's a bit odder to see intensely personal reactions to even standard directors. But it may be that a kind of California chauvinism has turned Didion into a nostalgic harkener back to defense of the studio days (in fact, much of her essay "In Hollywood" in *The White Album* is devoted to proving, or at least, asserting that the old Hollywood system still exists. Its demise, she says, is just a cliché—really a fantasy—of East Coast liberal reviewers who don't understand how the movie industry works.)

Didion is called a surf fascist by some residents of northern California because of her preference for old-time California values. In the essay on Hollywood, "I Can't Get That Monster Out of My Mind" (1964), her rancor is reserved not just for European directors, but also for the more au courant "modern" American film makers who insist on directing with a didactic purpose. About *Dr. Strangelove*, Didion decides that "rarely has so much been made over so little." Stanley Kramer, Carl Forman, and John Frankenheimer are also directors attacked because of their involvement with "issues" and "problems." It is clearly no accident that each of the films featured in the essay has a leftist-liberal tenor. Of all the movies in the creative and fertile cinematic field of the mid-1960s, it is not surprising that Didion discusses *Judgment at Nuremberg, The Victors* (a left-field choice, as is its director, Carl Forman) and Frankenheimer's *Seven Days in May.*

What these films have in common, according to Didion, is an "apparent calculation about what 'issues' are not safe—an absence of imagination, a sloppiness of mind in some ways encouraged by a comfortable feedback from the audience, from the bulk of reviewers, and from some people who ought to know better." The Europeans, Antonioni, Visconti, Fellini, Bergman, and Resnais, are demolished *in toto* in one paragraph, though each for a different reason.

What these films have in common, according to *this* reading, is that they stand for the kind of vaguely libertarian stuff that Didion is out gunning for. She shows her true colors at the end of the essay, in a paragraph that is separated from the rest of the piece and that relies on some not-so-clever non sequiturs: "We are no longer in the grip of a monster; Harry Cohn no longer runs Columbia like, as the saying went, a concentration camp. Whether or not a picture receives a Code seal no longer matters much at the box office. No more curfew, no more Daddy, *anything goes.* Some of us do not quite like this permissiveness; some of us would like to find "reasons" why our pictures are not as good as we know in our hearts they might be."

The obvious sentimentalism of this statement aside for the moment, the startling thing here is the polarity of "us" and "them." "They" are even more in evidence in her *White Album* piece, "In Hollywood." Although various Hollywood or industry-related scenarios are ironically presented, it is with the loving eye of the insider who knows the most revealing feature. The anger is kept for those who write about film, for the Kaels, the Kauffmanns, the Simons. In their insistence upon seeing corruption in Hollywood, and in not understanding the "circus" aspect—the collaborative quality of film making—they miss the boat entirely. But the entire matter is dismissed anyway in a clever hand-wave by Didion; reviewing films has a kind of "*petit-point*-on-Kleenex" effect that "rarely stands much scrutiny."

It's getting easier to see Didion's pieces as increasingly reaction-ary: Her tendency to refer to "my husband" throughout, as well as her distaste for anything smacking of liberal, or "east coast radical chic," values, are making her preferences predictable. Praising or dismissing movies according to one's political bent is not a trait peculiar to women writers (who would want to claim it?) as even a nodding acquaintance with the consistently liberal views of Stanley Kauffmann makes clear.

But for a writer with political proclivities and background, political and cultural connections can prove irresistible, almost obvious, as in the essays and reviews of Nora Sayre. Daughter of political reporter and screenwriter Joel Sayre, she grew up in Hollywood and around *New Yorker* writers, for which her father wrote. Blacklisted writers were "around the house" at a time when Sayre was coming to maturity, in the 1950s. After attending Radcliffe, Sayre became a political writer and columnist. She was a New York correspondent for awhile for *The New Statesman*, and while working on her 1973 collection of essays, *Sixties Going On Seventies*, was reviewing films for the *New York Times*. As of this writing Sayre occasionally reviews films for *The Nation*, and her second book *Running Time: Films of the Cold War* was recently pub-lished.

Perhaps because of an awareness of her political "heritage," Sayre makes political and cultural references a bit more ironically and less connectively. An excerpt from *Running Time*, which appeared in Sayre's film column in *The Nation*, notes the figure called the Bad Blonde. "In the 1950's," Sayre decides, "you knew that there was something terribly wrong with a woman if her slip straps showed through her blouse; in this context, it meant treason." As slyly, Sayre decides that communists have larger and blacker shadows, and walk with a forward slant that reveals their "dedication to their cause."

The ironic distance is retained even when Sayre uses a first-person intrusion, as we can see in her clever piece "Two New Films Focus on California and Californians" (a September 1, 1974 *Times* piece on *California Split* and *Chinatown*). "As a New Yorker," Sayre declares straightforwardly, "I return from every visit to California convinced that Manhattan is the most peaceful and rational of communities." Of course Sayre was reviewing for the *Times* from 1972–75, years when the impact of the earlier new journalism was beginning to make some in-roads into mainstream periodicals; therefore, the autobiographical refer-ence is not unexpected.

Sayre displays the same predilection for the most telling detail, to capture a particular culture: "Segal and Gould [in *California Split*] are comic versions of the wanderers—often failures—whom you constantly meet in California, the stragglers who swarm through motels and drive-ins and Pizzaburgers." As might be expected, films that Sayre either chose to review or was assigned to by the *Times* were frequently susceptible to political analysis, or background fill-in, like her 1975 review of *Les Violins du Bal* (this much-praised film, according to Sayre, "glamorized the persecution of the Jews") or of Charlie Chaplin's *A King In New York*, which explains the background of the film's suppression (it was released in Europe in 1957 but the American release was put off until 1973). Chaplin's politically allegorical comedy makes full and free use of the composite portrait of actor and part that is the recurrent thread in the writing of women film critics: it's OK, Sayre's review decides, for *A King in New York* to have a bitter ending, since Chaplin himself had such a hard time in America. And the even more personal detail that "Clearly, Chaplin loved playing King. Here, as in some of his other pictures, he seems to be in awe of the rich and the class system, though he has often derided both" (*New York Times*, October 22, 1973). A comparison with James Agee's review of Chaplin's 1947 *Monsieur Verdoux* makes the point, as the distinction between actor and part simply does *not* coalesce: we may "wonder why Chaplin's only direct statements, most of which are made through Verdoux, are so remarkably inadequate" (*The Nation*, June 21, 1947).

Seeing the actor's combined roles as ouevre and deciding that these parts affect the national psyche is a trait peculiar to women writers about film, as Sayre's piece, "Did Cooper and Stewart Have to Be So Stupid?" shows, for it rests on that premise. Male naifs who are *not* frontiersmen or woodsmen (in contradistinction to Perkins in the 1950s and Hoffman in the 1960s: also naifs, but intelligent ones), "proudly proclaim their stupidity. . . . Quite often reading seems difficult for them . . . But the back of their necks tingle when they hear the national anthem" (*New York Times*, August 7, 1977).

A talent for revealing the telling detail, the assumption of the cumulative effect of the actor's role on a nation, are characteristics of the woman film critic, but are particularly so for women culture critics. But it is Beauvoir, with typical comprehensiveness, who touches on the reasons that so many of the other properties of film criticism are attractive to women. Her criticism is extremely personal; it makes use of the amalgam of actor and role, as the quotes above show. But film's "potency of images" also overwhelms her, an illusion "I accept in a state of near-passivity." It provides Beauvoir with an occasion for vicarious experience, for power, and for omnipotence: "I slip silently into houses; I am present at events that cannot be seen. I sit by the bed upon which lovers make their love." And, too, "I pass through walls, I hover in the sky; I am endowed with supernatural powers" (*All Said and Done*).

8

The Writer's View:

Colette, Louise Bogan, Virginia Woolf,
Dorothy Richardson, Marianne Moore,
H.D., and Anaïs Nin

Of the many women who have written about film, none has had *less* of a professional interest than the women poets and fiction writers who were only occasionally tempted to the cinema. In this sense they are a "pure" test for devising a feminist aesthetic for film. Poets Marianne Moore, H.D. (Hilda Doolittle), and Louise Bogan were occasional writers on the cinema, as have been novelists Colette, Virginia Woolf, Anaïs Nin, and Dorothy Richardson. The writer's view—since the nineteenth century so recurrently the alternate, private, even solipsistic vision—is a perfect vehicle for women writing about an art that often seems to automatically elicit subjectivity. This is evident especially in the reviews of H.D. and Dorothy Richardson in their work for *Close Up,* the first film journal (published in the 1930s in England). But the trait common to these women writers is their extraordinarily evocative descriptions, and their efficacy with visual or telling detail.

In fact, if anything, being "close to the [creative] source" seems to have strengthened woman's abilities to detail, and to intellectually and emotionally "merge with" the actors, the individuals on the screen. For poet Anaïs Nin, the emotional—not the intellectual—apprehension of film art is what changes the viewer, thereby providing a kind of therapy. And in a literary age when imagism has nearly totally claimed poetry, and some would say the novel as well, efficacy with the visual or palpable detail is a given (less of an appeal, interestingly, is the narrative quality of mainstream films; novelists writing about the cinema seem to get no more or less caught up in plot explication or minutiae than other critics).

Naturally, not all writers find film irresistible. In our time only fiction writers Renata Adler and Penelope Gilliatt have attained national importance as film critics, and of contemporary male novelists writing about movies regularly only Graham Green has major status.[1]

Present-day poets do not seem drawn to film as in an earlier age; perhaps because contemporary women poets are more concerned with self-development and with "interpersonal" relationships. Poets Louise Bogan wrote an infrequent film piece for the *New Republic* in the 1920s, and H.D. and Marianne Moore wrote quite regularly on the cinema in the 1930s. The "occasional" article by a writer more well-known in another area is not uncommon; that Moore and H.D. cared to write about film regularly may seem more untoward. Yet *Close Up* was a forum for some of the most prominent intellectuals of its day. Published from 1927 to 1933 it was not coincidental that the journal had a leftist, even Marxist, orientation, with an editorial policy that demanded that film be considered from social, educational, and psychological points of view. (Bryher generally handled educational films for the journal.)

Coedited by writer and film maker Kenneth Macpherson and his then-wife Winifred Ellerman (the novelist who—as we have seen—published under the pseudonym Bryher, renaming herself in an attempt to dissociate herself from her publisher father's fortune, although he in fact kept the magazine afloat financially), *Close Up* attracted the foremost writers of its generation: Gertrude Stein and psychoanalysts Barbara Low and Havelock Ellis were just three who wrote for it. Bryher and H.D. were intimate friends, and there were other interconnections. Macpherson cast H.D. opposite Paul Robeson in his film about race relations, *Borderline,* and H.D. was herself interested in film making, and published poetry in *Close Up* about this activity. An American, H.D. lived most of her life abroad, having been married for a time to English poet Richard Aldington, and she had been an assistant editor of the British magazine *The Egoist.* Moore, the celebrated American poet and lifetime resident of Brooklyn, was born in 1887 and died in 1972. Her first book of poetry was published by the Egoist Press.

Yet more than these superficial commonalities, the shared impact of these poets' work on film is in their powers of description, especially their abilities with image. Marianne Moore—who once wanted to be a painter—uses her visually sensitive and observant qualities in the service of imagism. But it is a gift that perfectly transfers to film criticism. A review of *Lot in Sodom,* which appeared in the December 1933 *Close Up,* sees a sky with "wefts of cloud, a temple surrounded by buildings set together at various angles—greyed and unified in El Greco perspective." References to and analogies with painters are not unusual for film critics treating the visual, photographic, or "painterly" elements of the cinema, but there is a clear distinction between work written by women critics and criticism by their male counterparts. For Vachel Lindsay, another poet and critic who studied to be a painter, one analogy is to Botticelli: Mary Pickford "by some necromancy" must have appeared to the painter "in this phase of herself." Griffith's *Enoch Arden* contains a scene with happy children reminiscent of "many a genre painting on the theme of domesticity." But Lindsay's comparisons are more formal and less directly grafted on to the work under discussion.

In the same review by Moore of *Lot in Sodom,* the "high points are Lot's house—morning, with the blur of waving candle—flame on the undulating coarse-weave curtain; the glass-black blood quivering along a prostrate body; the glistening elaborate lily with snake-spots; the tortoise-shell spotted pallor of the snake with beady eyes." (Moore has always been noted for her references to nature and animals, so the fine adjectival descriptions in this review are a not unexpected—and nice—fillip.)

Yet documentaries provided the perfect joint for Moore's criticism. In a "round-up review" of some nature documentaries in the September 1933 *Close Up* called "Fiction or Nature?" there are "wild kangaroos in flight, undulating like the rapids of a dangerous stream." And while this description is not wildly poetic or literary, it can be advantageously compared with criticism by screenwriter and novelist Graham Greene, who wrote brief film reviews for both *The Spectator* and *Night and Day* (a kind of British *New Yorker*) from 1935-40. In describing a 1936 film, *Klio the Tiger,* Greene complains of the "horrid Technicolor browns and greens [which] stain the screen" but the review is remarkably lacking in visual description: "now we come to the wild animals, even the elephants, the pythons, the water-buffalo, 'most treacherous of horned beasts', present no so difficult dilemma." Greene is cleverly ironical, but there is neither the uniqueness of syntactical construction nor the unusualness of language that much criticism by women writers shows. The concentration on images, for instance, in H.D.'s review of Carl Dreyer's 1928 *The Passion of Joan of Arc* used to be known as "colorful," but more properly—in this case—is innovatively nonlinear and nonstandard. Jeanne d'Arc is presented to us "in a series of pictures, portraits burnt on copper, bronze if you will, anyhow obviously no aura of quattrocento gold and gold dust and fleurs-de-lys in straight hieractic pattern . . . but rather in hard clear line, remorseless, poignant, bronze stations of the cross, carved upon medieval cathedral doors."

It is a happy suspicion to think that the flashy "rightness" of description may be owing to an intensity of identification, and to an easy empathy with the object under review. For women critics to have such an ability is surely not odd, since the ready, even eager, yield of sympathy or sensibility—too often the hallmark of those without power—happens ironically to be the stamp of the fine critic, as well. And it at least partially explains H.D.'s extraordinary and extreme response to *The Passion of Joan of Arc.* The "reality" of Dreyer's Joan (played by Falconetti, who had never acted in a film before) causes the "spiritual antagonism I have to the shaved head, the stares, defiant bronze-statue." H.D. objects to viewing over and over again the "brute side of mystic agony." She is "wary," and "a little defiant" for, significantly, "not one of us is in need of this stressing and stressing, this poignant draining of hearts, this clarion call to pity."

This is a sophisticated response to the cinema from Doolittle, since it is by now an aesthetic commonplace that repeated images of violence may have the effect of banality ("Images anesthetize," says Susan Sontag in her book *On Photography*). "Do I have," Doolittle queries, "to be cut into slices by this inevitable pan-movement of the camera, these suave lines to the left, up, to the right, back all rhythmical with the remorseless rhythm of a scimitar? . . . I am shut in here. I want to get out. I want to get out." (*Close Up,* July 1928)

Finally, H.D. rhetorically asks "why must my very hands feel that they are numb and raw and bleeding, clenched fists tightened, bleeding as if bleating at those very impregnable medieval church doors?" The extremity of identification, the near coalescence, may seem erratic (and Doolittle here is its most impassioned, if seemingly overwrought, advocate), yet it must be said that the imaginative leaps have simply not been as forthcoming from male writers, Virginia Woolf's assertions about the creatively androgynous mind notwithstanding. A descriptive passage—otherwise quite keen and evocatively beautiful—by poet Vachel Lindsay makes the point: Blanche Sweet's Judith in *Judith of Bethulia* is "shown in her gray and silvery room in her former widow's dress, but not the same woman. There is thwarted love in her face. The sword of sorrow is there. But there is also the prayer of thanksgiving. She goes forth. She is hailed as her city's deliverer. She stands among the nobles like a holy candle." It may be argued that naturally a male writer would not so readily identify with an actress, but there is a similar distancing—a coolness—in Lindsay's description of an actor. Sessue Hayakawa, in both *The Clew* and *The Typhoon* for instance, "looks like all the actors in the old Japanese prints." (All Lindsay quotes are from *The Art of the Motion Picture*.) And one can feel the removal—almost a frame—even in a piece which declares itself to be over-involved, as James Agee's ironic, charming review of Elizabeth Taylor in *National Velvet* does: his admiration for her is as if he were in primary school, and her acting ability beside the point. Yet his review, which appeared in *The Nation* on December 23, 1944, is quite clear in its distinctions about Taylor's talent, which he believes she can turn "off and on much as she is told." He is hardly less than tongue-in-cheek when he declares "I think that she and the picture are wonderful, and I hardly know or care whether she can act or not."

Even a woman writer who is commenting negatively and apprehensively about film, as Virginia Woolf is for the most part in her essay,

"The Movies and Reality" (also called "The Cinema" is filled with an intensity owing to her subjectivity. The first (1927) film version of *Anna Karenina*, titled *Love*, with Greta Garbo, especially irritates Woolf. The voluptuous lady in black velvet is "no more Anna Karenina than it is Queen Victoria." For the "inside" of Anna's mind, "her charm, her passion, her despair" is not properly represented by teeth, pearls, and velvet. Woolf is angry in this piece, not just at this portrait of *Anna K.*, but—in the high cult vein—at the cinema in general (the piece begins "though people say that the 'savage' no longer exists in us, they have 'presumably forgotten the movies'").

Graham Greene's similar dislike for the slightly later version of *Anna Karenina* focuses on physical details too, but in a more austere fashion; Garbo's Anna has an "awkward ungainly body, her hollow face strong and rough as an Epstein cast." After observing that "she is more like a man than a woman" (a common comment among even contemporaneous critics) Greene decides that "what beauty she has is harsh and austere as an Arab's." This type of externalized description is most particularly and ingeniously put to use when—as might be expected with Greene—certain moral attributes are being pointed out. Thus the crisp, cool quality of his description of Fred Astaire: it needs, Greene declares,

> An effort of the mind to remember that Mr. Fred Astaire was not invented by a film director and drawn by a film draftsman. He is the nearest we are ever likely to get to a human Mickey, near enough for many critics to have noted the resemblance. If one needs to assign human qualities to this light, quick, humorous cartoon, they are the same as the early Mickey's; a touch of a courageous and impromptu intelligence, a capacity for getting into awkward situations. Something has to be done, and Mickey without a moment's hestitation will fling his own tail across an abyss and tread the furry unattached tightrope with superb insouciance. Something has to be done, and Mr. Astaire bursts into a dance which in its speed and unselfconsciousness seems equally to break the laws of nature.

> (A review of *Follow the Fleet*,
> in *The Spectator*, April 24, 1936.)

Greene is tops at light-hearted, elegant stylistic analysis, although any depth of emotional response may be missing. And when a physical observation *is* included, it's often a cooly startling epithet: what Greene is best at; that, for instance "Shirley Temple acts and dances with immense vigor and assurance, but some of her popularity seems to rest on a coquetry quite as mature as Miss Colbert's and on an oddly precocious body as voluptuous in grey flannel trousers as Miss Dietrich's." (*The Spectator*, August 7, 1936.) Colette is one writer, however, who combines a personal, moral standard with a profusion of physical details. She is associated with the cinema mainly in other ways. Colette's novels *Gigi* and *Cheri* have been adapted for the screen many times; but not as well known is the fact that she wrote screenplays, such as *Divine* (a 1935 film directed by Max Ophuls), *Lac-Aux-Dames* (1933), and—a movie that started to get revisionist attention in the mid-to-late-1970s—Leontine Sagan's 1932 *Maedchen in Uniform.*

Little publicized until recent years has been Colette's critical work, certainly not insignificant. Colette reviewed for three months for the "little magazine" *Le Film,* and in her by-lined column for *Le Matin* and *Excelsior* (from 1913-17) she periodically treated film. Other film essays are interspersed in Colette's collection of drama criticism, *La Jumelle Noire* (*Black Opera Glasses.*) But even within this very small critical corpus Colette has picked up cinematic elements that will prove to be extraordinarily important in the film-historical years to come. She is pioneer—and it may be said that in this she has no male counterpart—in pointing out a number of observations: the subtleties of black and white film as compared to color (she is in no rush for the color film, which she prophesys is on the way), the significance of cinematic realism as opposed to theatrical symbolism (and some early mistakes film made in this regard), the differences between stage and screen acting, and the importance of costume design. While she doesn't call it such, Colette notices the effects of quick cutting, predicts the coming takeover of the cinema by America, and offers a prescient analysis of the impact of Mae West that to this day has not been surpassed by any feminist critic. And she is a good "talent-spotter," picking up on unknown Mickey Rooney playing Puck in Max Reinhardt's *A Midsummer Night's Dream* (1935) and Sessue Hayakawa in *The Cheat* (1915).

Over all, Colette delicately, delightfully details. Compared to the "deep domain" of black and white, color has an "indiscreet clarity." One wonders if anyone but a poet or creative writer would come up with the unlikely word "indiscreet" in this context. And although the chilling effects of *film noir* or the startling contrasts of cinematic chiaroscuro are at her time not yet film traditions, Colette is able to foresee something along these lines as she worries what will happen to the "gripping contrast of shadow and light, psychological commentaries of incomparable eloquence." In fact, the piece is titled "Black and White."

The occasion for the essay is *A Midsummer Night's Dream.* Here the gradations of white are laid out with extraordinary and imaginative care and precision. In this film is the "white of pearls, the white of milk, the whitish-blue of the full moon, the whited gold of the rising sun-

. . . . Tiny white children, pathetic, with hair of frost; white lightning-bolts like a thousand fires . . . white of fog . . . fleshy petal-white of tube-roses." Colette has erased the line, in the old cliché, between literal and figurative description. In her review of Abel Gance's *Master Dolorosa,* too, there are scenes that are "lit with a rare richness—gilded whites, sooty and profound blacks."

Scene descriptions are not Colette's only forte when it comes to using the significant details she singles out. What makes the acting of Hayakawa so effective, for instance, is the "menace and disdain in a motion of his eyebrow," the "gesture of a hand" when his face may be mute, how the "ecstatic darkening of his eye" may convey "without shuddering, without convulsively grimacing that he has been wounded." The talent for subtleties required for screen acting makes a perfect joint with women's superior ability to cope with minutiae. Colette unabashedly makes an aesthetic point by using a "minor" detail to observe that "the bizarre and absurd detail of a dress design swept all before it, and the hearty Italian laugh burst out" (reviewing an unidentified "Roman cinema" in "Film and Fashion," June 35, 1917).

Perhaps best of all are the insights she manages about Mae West, quite possibly because the identification with West is so close. West's most significant trait, according to Colette, is her "impudence," a quality shared with Chaplin's various personae, and something that makes them both "solitary" (Colette may have meant "autonomous," a word that was not in vogue at the time). A star's autonomous control over a part or role could also be what Colette has in mind, for she declares that for such impudence to "ensure its survival" it finds itself obliged to "borrow the mask of simple grossness and a joviality that dishonors the dialogue. By means of such concessions, it remains an exclusively virile virtue." She hints here at an interpretation of actors as "working against the text" of a film that we see some present-day critics struggling for. According to Colette, West is even the "auteur and the principal interpreter of her films." (Quotes above are from "Les Cinéacteurs" in *La Jumelle Noire.*)

Something that particularly pleases Colette is that West has chosen or created parts in which not only is she alone, but she also avoids marriage, death, taking the "road to exile," bemoaning her passing youth, or feeling bitter at being abandoned. The conscious yearning to isolate a type, or a series of parts, in film seems exclusive to criticism by women writers. Moreover, it is touching to observe such a primitive, unaffectedly ingenuous craving for role models in women critics too early to function under the more structured feminism of recent years. While myriad writers have seen Garbo as an androgynous, angst-ridden mirror of the disjunctions of her age, poet Hilda Doolittle found in Garbo an alter-ego.

Doolittle, born in Pennsylvania in 1886, lived most of her life in Switzerland and died there in 1961. An intimate friend of the *Close Up* group, and a poet whose work is just now gaining esteem not only for its imagism but also for its discovery of some new feminine symbols and metaphors, H.D.'s involvement with film grew throughout her life. She contributed reviews and commentary to *Close Up,* and also two long poems, "Projector" and "Projector II (Chang)." In *Borderline,* a critically acclaimed 1930 film about race relations starring Paul Robeson (and directed by Kenneth Macpherson), she played opposite Robeson. She made three films of her own: *Wing Beat, Foothills,* and *Monkey's Moon* (the first two have been preserved).

H.D. complains that in Pabst's *Joyless Street* Garbo has been made to seem like a vamp, and that her "wigs, her eye-lashes have all but eclipsed our mermaid's straight state, her odd, magic quality of almost clairvoyant intensity." It is up to us to rescue her, H.D. decides in this piece, for Garbo is in reality a "captured innocent." When she first saw her, Garbo gave "a clue, a new angle, and a new sense of elation." And by the other side of the same coin, H.D.'s response to Garbo as Anna Karenina in *Love* is one of depressing deflation: she is here "inexpressively vulgar and incredibly dull" with a "lifeless and dough-like visage." It covers up what's *really* there: Garbo's "chiselled purity, the dazzling, almost unearthly body." In the insistence upon a direct knowledge, almost mystical communication with the actor/actress (and the critic is the only such one, this kind of writing implies) we see the same tendency that later pervades the work of Pauline Kael, for one. The width of such a leap mainly betrays a deep emotional need.

Although H.D.'s critical work is laden with fanciful images, such as Garbo as a "nordic ice-flower," she is not weak in theoretical apprehension. It is the censor, Doolittle insists, who forces a woman to be either a "vamp" or an "evil woman." And *if* a vamp, the actress must be "black-eyed, must be dark." In 1927, this is way before the dark-light virgin-whore dichotomy so perfectly spelled out in Leslie Fiedler's *Love and Death in the American Novel.* And H.D. is also in advance of Cocteau's famous quote comparing the cinema to a temple, with its sacrificial victims. In the final part of her three-part essay, "The Cinema and the Classics," the "cinema palace . . . became a sort of temple." And she wonderfully analyzes the hypnotic effects and aspects of film: "We moved like moths in darkness, we were hypnotized by cross currents and interacting shades of light and darkness and maybe cigarette smoke. . . . We sank into this pulse and warmth and were recreated."

Novelist Dorothy Richardson is just as aware of the audience while writing her regular column "Continuous Performance" for *Close Up.* For leftist or socialist criticism such concern for the audience may seem a natural by-product; it may be seen as another offshoot of women's learned or innate sensitivity to others, as well. Particularly memorable is Richardson's description of a movie audience in a rural town where there were "tired women, their faces sheened with toil, and small children, penned in semi-darkness and foul air on a sunny afternoon. There was almost no talk. Many of the women sat alone, figures of weariness at rest. Watching these I took comfort. At last the world of entertainment had provided for a few pence, tea thrown in, a sanctuary for mothers, an escape from the everlasting *qui vivre* into eternity on a Monday afternoon." She sees too the vicarious relief afforded by that "simple music," resulting in the "shining eyes and rested faces of those women." (*Close Up*, July 1927)

Music is a natural area of attention for Richardson, since much of her work for *Close Up* is concerned with finding an aesthetic for the silent film, as opposed to the "talkies." For Richardson, author of the multi-volume autobiographical work-in-progress *Pilgrimage*, a work in—in the term she preferred—"interior monologue," the early silent film approximates a "feminine" form. Film was superior in "the day of its innocence, in its quality of being nowhere and everywhere, nowhere in the sense of having more intention than direction and more purpose than plan, everywhere by reason of its power to evoke, suggest, reflect, express from within its moving parts and in their totality of movement, something of the changeless being at the heart of all becoming, was essentially feminine."

Unfortunately, with the advent of the talkies, film is changing and "becoming audible and particularly in becoming a medium of propaganda, it is doubtless fulfilling its destiny," according to Richardson. "But it is a masculine destiny. The destiny of planful becoming rather than of purposeful being. It will be the chosen battleground of rival patterns, plans, ideologies in endless succession and bewildering varieties." Richardson dreads such "straight-line thinkers" who are "occidental" (one can divine her differentiation with more "creative" thinking being "oriental" and "feminine") and who are usually found "believing in the relative passivity of females." Psychology, according to Richardson, supports her suspicions: it, like the silent film, is on the side of "feminine thinking." "Memory, psychology is today declaring, is passive consciousness . . ." not the "mere glance over the shoulder along a past seen as a progress from the near end of which mankind goes forward." Many film theorists have posited that because of its undisturbed visual purity the silent film is superior to the sound film, though none have tied this belief to any other theoretical significance. (Quotes above from various *Close Up* volumes, 1932.)

All this theory—and *Close Up* is interesting if in no other way than for watching the impromptu accommodation of theory to the leaps and jumps of a five-year era of extraordinary change in the cinema—does not preclude some of the inventiveness of description that runs through work by women writers. In her September 1929 column "Dialogue in Dixie," Richardson tells us that some of the characters in the film have mouths that open "like those of fish, like those of ventriloquists' dummies." In a piece titled "Captions," which discusses this topic in relation to the silent film, Richardson complains of unidimensional actors whose "pulpy rouged mouths are forever pouting, folding, parting in a smile that laboriously reveals both rows of teeth" (September 1927).

Anaïs Nin is probably the most persuasive of all critics-*cum*-writers. However, in defending and explaining her method, she presents perhaps the quintessence of a "feminine" approach. In her essay, "Ingmar Bergman," Nin recommends that the emotional content of a film be zeroed in on directly. It is a compliment from Bergman, she asserts, that he doesn't always bother to make logical or analytical sense out of his films: he "honors your intelligence by leaving the interpretation to you." By presenting the extremes of emotional experiences, which we as Westerners tend to avoid, Bergman hopes to help us undergo a change of some sort. He, Bergman, asks "you to *suffer* it, because he knows that if you do not enter experience with emotion, but only with the mind, it will not change you."

And by concentrating on only a few people, and by using music, Bergman bypasses analysis and "brings us into intimate contact with a few people." In *Cries and Whispers,* for instance, we "become intimate as never before with the process of dying. We become intimate with the meaning of compassion," etc. Nin here credits John Simon with the concept of the "chamber film," taken from the intensely focused chamber music, although Susan Sontag, in her 1967 essay on *Persona,* predates Simon. Maya Deren was the very first to propose the concept and phrase, in a *Village Voice* guest column of August 25, 1960. However, she means it for the avant-garde or underground film (as a mainstream narrative film would be like a ninety-piece orchestra).

In this essay Nin nicely weaves her own notions about psychoanalysis, dreaming, and the emotive theory of art (it is "the emotional, not the analytical, journey which brings deliverance from secret corrosions"). Bergman may seem obviously—if perfectly—suited to the writer, who has continually probed emotion and her own unconscious in her work, who has insisted upon the importance, and difference, of femininity, even as she herself became a feminist heroine and prophet. And in a 1965 review of Jean Genêt's *Un Chant d'Amour* Nin delights in just the sort of imagistic description she finds in Bergman; one that invites participation from the observer: in the film's "most sadistic moment, a prisoner being whipped by a guard dreams of woodlands, sunlight, and pagan fulfillment. It is the guard who, unable to attain this, can only wield a gun as a symbol of virility, can only destroy because he is incapable of desire." And of course a writer's imaginative sensibility can inform a description: there is the "exchange of symbolic acts: pushing a straw through the prison wall, breathing the smoke of a cigarette as a carrier of the breath of desire, swinging flowers from window to window just beyond the reach of thirsty hands. What casts a shadow of ugliness in other films results from the attitude and vision of the film maker. Puritanism paints in ugly colors. Here the Negro's priapic dance in his cell untainted by hypocrisy assumes the stature of a pagan ritual."

For women writers, film provided more than an escape, more than a mere diversion from their "real" work. Notions about art, about creativity, are often worked through in the criticism of women, as are some of the same themes that run through their novels and poetry. An already finely honed descriptive ability combines with an extraordinary sensitivity to the actors or characters in movies, in this sense the most "personal," the most kinetic of all the arts.

NOTE

1. James Agee's Pulitzer Prize winning novel *A Death in the Family* was, after all, published posthumously in 1951; throughout his lifetime it was the critical work for which Agee was most well-regarded.

Conclusion

While not all the characteristics that have been discussed belong across-the-board to all women film critics it is true that there are a number of theoretical positions that emerge. Nearly all the women critics presented here insist upon the extreme influence of the star upon the audience and/or the culture, the work of the actor-actress as a whole or ouevre, and confuse—some deliberately and some without apparent forethought—individual actors and actresses with the parts they played. There is a tendency to personalize in near total identification with star, audience, and even director. Almost all women film critics, too, are extraordinarily fine with and attentive to details, both in their own work and in citing the work of others.

These theoretical positions seemed to arise readily and naturally in analyzing the work of women film critics. It is best, one hopes and knows, when theory develops *from* the material rather than the other way around. Still, and interestingly, a number of recent research findings in women's studies and the psychology of sex differences—particularly those involving perception and cognition—are in support of the "special" point of view suggested here. At the risk of leaping in where others have feared to tread, I will list those conclusions that pertain directly to film viewing by women. More than men, women have been found to be more sensitive to music, to certain visual stimulus, and to social interchange. They are more visually sensitive in the dark,[1] better at facial recognition and more responsive to faces,[2] and more sensitive than men to sound when they are sleeping (if the dream-film analogy can apply here).[3]

The most startling discovery for me about women's perceptual proclivities has been women's reactions to a standard psychological test called the rod and frame test: in complete darkness, surrounded by a luminous frame, women found it difficult to separate an independent rod from its frame: therefore, psychologists have determined that they are more field dependent than men are.[4] Applied to film criticism, this suggests the strong perception of part to whole and may be the cognitive underpinning for the concept of performer as auteur as well as the meld of actor or actress with part played. It is a precept now filtering down to popular journalism. Janet Maslin observes, for instance, "if an actress's character can shape her screen roles, the opposite can also be true" and of June Allyson, that there's "no separating her public and private personalities" (a review of two memoirs by June Allyson and Louise Brooks, *New York Times*, July 11, 1982).

Women's fears that their abilities with detail would consign them to a lifetime of tatting have been alleviated by studies that show that this tactile superiority transfers to other realms.[5] Even those critics, for instance, who tend to paint with a broad brush, like Iris Barry, have an aesthetic that is based on appreciating the significant detail. Close-ups of natural elements, particularly in Griffith's films, are what delight Barry the most. With typical insouciance she can declare that it is "not quite true to say 'And then came D.W. Griffith with the close-up' but it is useful"; particularly wonderful, too, are his close-ups of hands in *Intolerance*. Finding just the right detail in films is mirrored in women film critics' own writing, which so very often comes up with the right, palpable element. This ability can be observed across the decades, from critics as early as C.A. Lejeune to today's Janet Maslin. A Maslin piece in the *New York Times* on 1982s *Shoot the Moon*, for instance, captures the funky elegance of northern California: "When Diane Keaton romps with her lover, played by Peter Weller, she does it stylishly, aboard a tractor" (Maslin's point here is that director Alan Parker is good on surface things although not so great on character motivation). For the Sunday London *Times* critic Dilys Powell it is in fact the "richness of detail" that makes the cinema so endlessly fascinating.

Other women film critics are more chronologically oriented, often by decades. This approach stresses the impact of film stars on the surrounding culture, and the critics perceive themselves as representative of the culture in their response to or interaction with certain stars. The film criticism of the 1930s provides a bedrock here, as critics like Bryher and Richardson hopefully insist that the cinema will provide social change. The conscious, sometimes desperate, search for role models and suitable films—one of the more touching aspects of feminist film criticism—can be seen in the work of early polemicists as impassioned as Bryher and Richardson, but also in the writing of Lejeune and Barry (though for the former it is, as well, the vicarious relief from the tedium of everyday lives that the cinema provides for its less fortunate viewers). A similar emotional intensity colors some of the writing of feminist critics Haskell and Mulvey, yet the not infrequent insertion of self as vessel, conductor, or at least cultural seismograph could not have taken place without the somewhat earlier willful, sometimes naive self-insertion of critics such as Kael, Didion, Gilliatt, even Beauvoir, acting as a journalistic style bridge by incorporating first-person tactics and techniques of autobiographical (or new) journalism. Naturally the first-person intrusion is to be found in the critical work of men, too, but they need *not* meet the urgent need of identification or vicarious escape (they have no such pressing demand).

In fact, the connections of women writers and critics with film may be divided into two areas: why they are drawn to the cinema, and what they bring to its criticism. I have suggested earlier that women were attracted to an entertainment form that was cheap, readily accessible, and that had no complicated social machinery surrounding it. The democratic origins of film provide some proper underpinnings here, and the reactions of writers as different as Iris Barry, Susan Sontag, and Annette Michelson demonstrate that varied intellects and sensibilities are attracted to an art with its roots in mainstream culture. Barry's introduction to *Let's Go to the Movies* makes subtle fun of the snobbery against this lowbrow art form: "At the moment we are a little ashamed of ourselves. Critics and connoisseurs demonstrate their deep sense by damning the films in every key. So those of us who go to the pictures every week, or every day, keep it rather quiet, or allude to it as being cheap, or restful. Others of us even allege that it solves our complexes. Going to the pictures is nothing to be ashamed of. I should like to discuss why we do slink into the cinema and what happens to us there." The year is 1926. Yet nearly a half-century later, Sontag can declare in a short piece, "A Note on Novels and Films," collected in *Against Interpretation*, that the origins of fiction and film are the same. The figures she follows through are novelist Richardson and director Griffith, with their similarly "vulgar" examination of emotion and sensibility as expressed through their heroines such as Pamela, Clarissa, and the Gish sisters. Of course Sontag moves to the side of this position, subtly satirized in "Theatre and Film," that once one accepts film as a democratic art, the "preeminent art of mass society," the wish is for movies to "continue to reflect their origins in a vulgar level of the arts, to remain loyal to their vast unsophisticated audience. Thus a vaguely Marxist orientation collaborates with a fundamental tenet of romanticism. Cinema, at once high art and popular art, is cast as the art of the authentic" (*Styles of Radical Will*). With Sontag's concern for surface or sensory values, it's a fast aesthetic jump for the avant-garde or experimental film to be equated with poetry. (And in her protean ability to take all critical positions one may see Sontag as truly ingenious, or else as without shame.) Still, she does not turn her back on the original concept of the mass appeal of films. Annette Michelson is more singularly, if tortuously, connective in tying the avant-garde film to radical possibilities that can or might change society. In shaking us up visually (consider Sontag's notion that all truly great art makes us "nervous"), Michelson asserts that we will rethink Western patriarchal values. Yet if social change will result, she still does not solve the problem of the limited audience to which such films might appeal. It is a slightly different version of the same problem—to my mind as yet unsolved—that would face feminist critics of a few years later, in their attempt to apply a semiological analysis to mainstream film as a way of deconstructing the text as well as defusing the Hollywood patriarchal system and narrative films. It is a nice curiosity that it is mainly British critics—Mulvey, Cook, and Johnston, et al.—who are attracted to this method. (Keeping both method and subject more generally sociological, American feminist critics have stuck to a more simple-minded sociological approach, even though by pointing out proper and improper role models their goal is a similar one—to change society. Though some, like Marsha Kinder of USC, also hope to alter the structure of films as a means to that end.)

The "democratic" origins of film is a critical commonplace and go some way toward explaining the attraction of women, a majority with little power, to the cinema. I have also suggested that reviewing—a form less codified and rigid than either essays or books—may have a particular appeal for women, for it need not have the patriarchal or Germanic linearity of other literary forms. For instance, the reviews of Cecelia Ager for *Vogue* in the 1930s discuss *only* the women stars and most frequently only their clothing. Pieces, as we have seen, by Kael and Gilliatt are widely, wildly different in both style and content. Lest we think this is mainly because of the latitude afforded by *The New Yorker,* we can also look to reviews as different as those by Adler, Sayre, and Maslin, all written for the *New York Times.* And despite what Virginia Woolf has said in her essay on reviews about the space, time, and informational limitations and considerations of reviewing, it should be clear to us—after only a cursory look at the work of a Dorothy Richardson, or the "occasional" character and quality of a piece by Susan Sontag on film—that the review, particularly for the little magazine or periodical, actually need have no such limitations at all (Woolf after all was concentrating on a certain type of deadlined Fleet Street journalism written to formula; moreover, she was discussing book reviewing.)[6] Only in one sense is it more chronologically bound than other forms of criticism: the informality of tone allows it to reflect the style and prejudices of each respective age or decade. So the quaintness of Iris Barry is matched by the sometimes cutesy qualities of the 1930s style: one may look at the film reviews of Helen Lawrenson for *Vanity Fair,* as well as the previously mentioned Ager reviews. The insistence upon "gaiety" is in gen-

eral the signpost of the style of the 1930s and early-1940s, as we can see
in the writing of their British counterpart C.A. Lejeune, for instance:
"Little can prudently be said about *Cobra Woman.* Sabu and Jon Hall
are in it, and Maria Montez comes in two styles: sinister, in the regalia of
an island queen, and simple in the Technicolor sarong of blameless maid-
enhood." (A review of *Cobra Woman* titled, "For This Relief—Much
Thanks," 1944.)

Perhaps enough has been said about the sleep-like qualities of film
as noticed by a majority of women critics and reviewers, from Barry to
Magny to Michelson, from Powdermaker to Adler, the private, dark,
dreamy attributes of cinema-going have been spoken about. Yet it is
Maya Deren who moves this perception most smoothly into the realm of
critical aesthetic; in her guest film column for the *Village Voice* she declares: "Criticism requires an objective receptivity, an awareness of and
sensitivity to another man's statement to a degree which is virtually a
form of passivity" (July 14, 1960). I have suggested that this passivity,
or really empathy as it is here described, has to do with women's receptivity to the moods of others. And if the darkened theater, the sleep-like
aura, releases psychic demons by its available symbolism (or as Barry
would lightheartedly call them, "our complexes,") it is as valid to observe that the barriers of everyday civilized life are removed as we are—
men and women alike—made more vulnerable, more susceptible, to the
faces and experiences on the screen. For women critics, as we see in their
extraordinary sensitivity to the work of certain actors, directors, even
their awareness of the audience, the emotional openness goes beyond
sensitivity, or sensibility. Intuition is a word that is disparaged today
(and no wonder, for it was our boon in lieu of rational achievement). It
has been conjectured here that woman's quickness in catching the
moods and innuendoes of others has had to do with being part of the
group or the class that is not in power. As a learned response she had to
be able to quickly pick up on the moods of others. And recent research is
deciding that—indeed—women more than men directly define their
actions according to the responses of other people, not of principles or
rules.[7]

The implications for film criticism are wide, if not startling. The
empathetic flow can lead to direct discoveries, as we see in the criticism
of Colette; here "finding" Sessue Hayakawa: "when his face is mute, his
hand carries on the flow of his thought . . . in the instant when he is
wounded, he creates the impression that his life is running out with his
blood, without shuddering." For Anaïs Nin, for whom a certain film is
an "X-ray of our psychic life," it is through the emotional, not intellectual apprehension that film can change, affect, alter the viewer (her comments on Bergman are especially full in this regard). Even a critic as
"rational" as Beauvoir defends her emotional response to films by say-

ing that thereby she can partake of other experiences, other lives.

These special gifts that women film critics bring to their craft go in two directions: empathetic understanding (here we might think of the work of Gilliatt, of H.D.). And it also betrays the yearning for power that manifests itself in vicarious identification, as expressed in the work of Kael or theorized about by Sontag. It is a perhaps too-sly suggestion to say that the reason their criticism is so compelling is that it is responding to power.

Some of the direct results of these motivations for film criticism and reviewing have been variations of auteur theory for directors and for actors and actresses. My own explanation for an "early" discovery of an auteur theory for directors turns on woman's conditioned, learned readiness to confer the title or denomination "master" to male creators. One conjectures that it was relatively easy to spot a cinematic Beethoven by being attuned to the nuances of his style. My conclusion holds that C.A. Lejeune was the chronological pioneer of either sex, as I have tried to show, in pointing out in the *Observer* that Chaplin, in 1941, is a director "whose signature on the film represents final and incomparable authority." In 1943, also for the *Observer,* we have similarly noted a review of Orson Welles's *The Magnificent Ambersons,* "If you don't happen to care about style, but simply want to get on with the story and find out who marries whom and who did what, this is not the work for you. Mr. Welles is one of the few directors who scrawls his signature across every scene. He accepts no ukases nor conventions; he sets his cameras roaming to find the new approach to the old situation; he will shoot an actor from the roof, the basement or the coal-shuttle if the fancy takes him; the sound track gives him a free world to range in. As far as he is concerned, there might not have been half a century of cinema already. For him, the film medium is now, and just beginning; a fresh page for him to cover with his bold characteristic handwriting." Even more explicitly, a review of *A Night at the Opera* concludes:

> A great number of people may contribute towards the final achievement, but they work best when they have a strong personality to hold them together. Orson Welles is a creator of that temper; so is Noel Coward; Alfred Hitchcock is another; so is Preston Sturges. You may like the work of Messrs. Welles, Coward, Hitchcock, and Sturges, or you may loathe it, but it is emphatically their own work; you will never confound it with the work of Messrs. Smith, Brown, Jones, and Robinson. These men scrawl their signature across a film so boldly that no one can fail to read it. The same rule applies to the Marx Brothers, more than to any other comedians since Chaplin. Groucho, Harpo, and Chico may be your delight or your anathema, but once seen—some will say endured—they are never forgotten; their three-fold personality has produced a type of comedy that is

unique on the screen. ("More About the Marx," 1945)

While the three-part structure of Andrew Sarris's auteur theory may not be formally stated, there is nonetheless a similar emphasis on the uniqueness of the director's vision, an insistence on the fact that he [sic] dominates all aspects of the making of the film, and that his "stamp" is to be discerned in all of this work. As has been previously noted, books by Bryher as well as Lejeune, Magny, and Eisner have auteur premises, declarations, and book divisions, from 1929 up through the 1950s.

It has become obvious to me that women critics and reviewers, as generous as they are in calling attention to screenwriters (Kael and Magny come to mind) or to editors (here it is Kael), have been absolutely predominant in seeing the work of an actor or actress as oeuvre, or in delineating the auteur-like character of many performers. In their distinction between those who have it and those who don't we see the structure for an aesthetic of acting, or a sense of acting as amalgam in—surprisingly—Magny, Lejeune, Colette, Trilling, Beauvoir, Kael, Gilliatt, and all the feminist critics. Some even come out for a willed or conscious selection of parts by the actors and actresses themselves. And, legitimately or not, a few, like Kael, Didion, Rosen, and Haskell, confuse the part with the player. In her comments about Mae West, Colette makes use of the word auteur (naturally she was writing in her native French, but the notion of author is the same in either language and has been retained by the translator). Perhaps more important, she is "the principal interpreter of her films." The year is 1934. Colette is definite on one point, however: the "real" Mae West is not the same as the persona of the films, even if it is West we refer to over and over again.

Nearly 40 years later, feminist Joan Mellen will use this sense of West as delineator of her cinematic fortune in outlining some thematic constants in West's film roles: her difficult or "masculine" vocations, and her domination over the men in her life. As we have seen, feminists Rosen and Haskell posit many of the same ideas about West and other stars. Lejeune has similar assumptions about Chaplin, Pickford, and others; Magny distinguishes between those with and those without such "star" quality: "An excellent interpretative artist like Bette Davis has never been able to raise herself to the level of star," never—unlike Garbo, Chaplin, and West—been able to crystallize around herself a web of collective representations, precisely because she has too plastic a personality, too great a mimetic gift. She does not have an existence of her own" (*The Age of the American Novel*). For Magny, as mentioned earlier, it is the carry-over of dominant physical and personal characteristics of some—like Katharine Hepburn or Joan Crawford—that gives them "star" personality, or lends them a mythic aura. And with descriptive criticism that borders on aphoristic cultural brilliance, Simone de Beauvoir uses the oeuvre assumption, highlighting physical details, to underpin her essay on Brigitte Bardot, as all of Bardot's roles are called upon at will to demonstrate a different aspect of Bardot's persona, and of her paradigmatic relationship with French middle-class society.

We have seen how critics Marjorie Rosen and Molly Haskell used physical details for many purposes: to stress a cultural stereotype, to comment on the individual star embodying the role, and to include the critic's own personal identification, thus making herself a spokesperson for society-at-large. The role of fantasy, of vicarious identification, is key here. For critic Pauline Kael, too, as her gleaming piece on Cary Grant shows, is able to move the dotted line between actor, role, and entire career at will, and always to her advantage (why not?) You know she may "know better," but she just goes ahead with fanzine melding whenever it suits her. And, as we have seen, the same holds true for directors. It's as if Kael had decided at the last minute, in the kind of montage criticism at which she is so clever, to cast them in their own picture. It may have to do with their personalities as well as their flashy journalistic style and times, but both Kael and Joan Didion make dramatic use of self-insertion and the assumed conjunction of individual and part played.

What might be the biggest surprise of all in examining the work of women film critics is to find their bellwether work in regard to the character of various national cinemas. The European critics, as we have seen, have been the most prescient in this regard, possibly because Americans in general either take the whole world as their province or else stick more specifically to their own local roots. In their heightened awareness of others women film critics have readily picked up on various national styles and characteristics. Eisner, Houston, and Bryher are particularly fine, as we have seen, in pinpointing certain qualities of the German, French, and Soviet cinemas, respectively. Houston, Dawson, and Gilliatt are quite good on the American film, and both Houston and C.A. Lejeune spot trends and motifs in their own national cinema. For Houston, at the time of *The Contemporary Cinema* it was the 1960s redbrick socialism; Lejeune in the 1940s uses Noel Coward for a kind of convenient slotting: a footnote to her 1945 review of *Brief Encounter* declares: "The point is that these Coward films are probably the nearest things we have to a valid modern school in British cinema. They are not only fine pieces of work, but fine pieces of native work. They are as full of British allusion as a volume of Punch, a Sullivan tune, or a Muirhead Bone drawing. You often hear people say, 'Why can't we make films over here with the taste, and art, and honesty of the French cinema?' In his own way, and in his own idiom, Coward does."

There is one awkward question that cannot go unanswered in a book even as unabashedly partisan as this has been. It's not exactly in the vein of the old saw about the female Shakespeares, but one might raise a correlative point with Shaw in mind. While there are women film critics who share his best qualities: wit that does not get in the way of principles, aesthetic concerns that do not dim the enthusiasm of the moment, he has no peer as both critic and creator. (Although the relationship of the "creative" artist to criticism is not a subject to go into at length here.) For Shaw, for one (Coleridge may be another, yet Shaw is the better example since he is working in a popular form of "entertainment") one energy or activity did not siphon off the other. Yet Susan Sontag can admit that after making films of her own she felt less inclined to criticize the work of others.[8] And Maya Deren, the avatar of the avant-garde film, watches subtle shifts in the writings of a fellow critic to decide that when he starts to make his own films, aesthetic principles that were important to him as a critic transmute to larger concerns of "truth" and documentary reality.[9] Also in the "loose ends" category we might consider the inspirational impact of critic and curator Lotte Eisner on the work of film makers, one obvious case in point being Werner Herzog's "walk" from Munich to Paris with his film *Kasper Hauser* strapped to his back in "protest" at Eisner's heart attack in 1980. (The adoration is not a chivalric one, for one thinks of Keat's walking tour when he hoped to find and visit Wordsworth.) Still within the European tradition, but with the added dimension of publicity: that layer that has made all of film art seem "tainted" by commercialism.

In finding a vehicle for their suppressed power needs, in latching on to an art form that provides an outlet for intense identification with others, women film critics have made film their very own. But as the luxuriance of their work shows, they are happy to give it back again, with interest.

NOTES

1. Diane McGuiness, "Perception and Cognition," *Exploring Sex Differences,* Lloyd and Archer, eds. (New York: Academic Press, 1976), p. 131.

2. M. Lewis et al., "Infants' Response to Facial Stimuli During the First Years of Life," *Developmental Psychology* I (1969), pp. 75–86.

3. McGuiness, p. 130.

4. Witkin et al., *Psychological Differentiation: Studies of Development* (New York: John Wiley, 1962), p. 2. In this context, see Helen Lambert's Comments on Witkin, in "Biology and Equality: A Perspective on Sex Differences" (Signs, Vol. 4, no. 1, autumn 1978). The relative "passivity" of women—an important component of the film experience—is taken up in E.E. Macoby's *The Development of Sex Differences* (Stanford, Calif: Stanford University Press, 1966, pp. 44-47).

5. McGuiness, p. 141.

6. Virginia Woolf, "Reviewing," in *The Captain's Death Bed and Other Essay* (New York: Harcourt, Brace 1950).

7. See Carol Gilligan's *In A Different Voice* (Cambridge, Mass.: Harvard University

Press, 1982).

8. Interview with Susan Sontag, *New York Times,* October 11, 1970.
9. Maya Deren, guest column *Village Voice,* July 14, 1960.

Selected Annotated Bibliography

This bibliography assumes a working knowledge of film history and theory. Works that are pertinent to this study and/or new in the field have been included.

ADLER, RENATA

Books

A Year in the Dark: Journal of a Film Critic 1968–1969 (New York: Random House, 1969). A collection of Adler's *New York Times*reviews.

Reviews

Appeared in *The New Yorker,* fall 1979, passim.

Articles

"The Sad Tale of Pauline Kael," *New York Review of Books,* August 14, 1980. A review of Kael's *When the Lights Go Down,* which concludes that all of Kael's work is sexually violent or scatological. Depends on textual analysis of Kael's language.

AGER, CECILIA

Reviews

Appeared in *Vogue* during the 1930s. Some of Ager's reviews are collected in *Garbo and the Nightwatchmen,* Alistair Cooke, ed. (New York: McGraw-Hill, 1971).

BARRY, IRIS

Curator, reviewer, critic, and historian. Founder of the film department at New York's Museum of Modern Art; lecturer at Columbia University; book reviewer for the New York *Herald Tribune.*

Books

Let's Go to the Movies (New York: Arno, 1972); reprint of 1926 edition published in London by Payson and Clarke titled *Let's Go to the Pictures.* Enormously popular general introduction to films (Barry would have preferred "movies"). Designed for and appreciated by a general readership.

D. W. Griffith: American Film Master (New York: Museum of Modern Art, 1940). A pioneer work; culmination of Barry's curatorial work at MOMA. It went out of print shortly after publication, but was reissued in 1965 by MOMA with annotated list of films by Eileen Bowser.

Reviews and Articles

Have appeared in *Sight and Sound, Home and Food, Town and Country, Vogue,* and *Hollywood Quarterly.*

General

Foreword to *The Film Index*, compiled by Barry et al. for the WPA Writer's Project (New York: MOMA and H.W. Wilson, 1941).

Preface to *Rise of the American Film*, by Lewis Jacobs (New York: Teachers College Press, 1968). Includes Barry's essay "Experimental Cinema in America, 1921–1942."

Film Notes: the Program Notes for the Film Library Circulating Program, MOMA, 1935–40.

Notes and Bulletins, including the first MOMA Bulletin; various pamphlets, 1935–39. Special issue: "The Silent Film," 1949 *Film Notes:* Part One.

Trans. *History of Motion Pictures*, by Maurice Badèche and Robert Brasillach (New York: W.W. Norton, 1938).

BARTHES, ROLAND

"The Face of Garbo" (1957), in *Film Theory and Criticism: Introductory Readings*, compiled by Gerard Mast and Marshall Cohen (New York: Oxford University Press, 1979).

BAZIN, ANDRÉ

What is Cinema?, Vol. I, Hugh Gray, trans.; and Vol. II, Hugh Gray, trans. and comp. (Berkeley: University of California Press, 1979).

DE BEAUVOIR, SIMONE

Books

Brigitte Bardot and the Lolita Syndrome (New York: Arno, 1972); reprint of 1960 edition.

All Said and Done, Patrick O'Brian, trans. (New York: Putnam, 1974). Beauvoir's autobiography; the fourth volume contains film reviews and criticism.

BOWSER, EILEEN

Current curator of the Museum of Modern Art.

Books

D. W. Griffith: American Film Master, by Iris Barry, with annotated list of films by Eileen Bowser (New York: Museum of Modern Art, 1965).

Monograph: "The Films of Carl Dreyer" (New York: Museum of Modern Art, 1964).

Reviews and Articles

Have appeared in the *New York Times* and *Films in Review*, often covering "lost" or rediscovered films.

General

Film Notes, ed. Eileen Bowser. Revised and expanded earlier *Film Notes* 1935–49. Especially notable are Bowser's good comments on De Sica's *Two*

Women included in "A Major Gift: Seven Films Acquired Through Joseph Levine."

BROOKS, LOUISE

Lulu in Hollywood (New York: Alfred Knopf, 1982). Reflections on her experiences there, with the industry and other movie stars. Strong on Gish, Garbo, and Bogart. Afterword by Lotte Eisner. Sections published previously in *Film Culture, Sight and Sound, Image, The New Yorker.* Brooks reportedly burned her earlier autobiography. Famous essay on Brooks is by Kenneth Tynan, *The New Yorker,* 1979.

BRYHER [Winifred Ellerman]

Books

The Heart to Artemis: A Writer's Memoirs (New York: Harcourt, Brace and World, 1962). Includes good comments on the founding of *Close Up,* husband and coeditor Kenneth Macpherson, friend and occasional lover H.D. Reflections on Germany and the Soviet Union in the 1930s; an unexpected portrait of Eisenstein.
Film Problems of Soviet Russia (Territet, Switzerland: Pool, 1929).

Reviews and Articles
Appeared in *Sight and Sound* and *Close Up* (1927–33), of which Bryher was coeditor. *Cinema Survey* by Herring, Bryher, Bower (London: Blue Moon Press, 1937); "Films in Education" by Bryher.

CAMERA OBSCURA

Collectively edited journal devoted exclusively to the study of women and film, founded in Los Angeles in 1974.

COLETTE

Film reviews appeared in the "little" magazine *Le Film* and newspapers *Le Matin* and *Excelsior,* during the years 1913–17. Her drama criticism appeared in *La Jumelle Noire* in 1935.

COOK, PAM

British feminist structuralist. Her work appears mainly in *Screen,* notably "Exploitation Films and Feminism," (summer 1966). Also, with Claire Johnston, "The Place of Women in the Films of Raoul Walsh," in *Raoul Walsh,* Phil Hardy, ed. (Edinburgh Film Festival, 1974). "Approaching the Works of Dorothy Arzner," in *The Work of Dorothy Arzner,* Claire Johnson, ed. (London: BFI, 1975).

CRIST, JUDITH

Books
The Private Eye, The Cowboy, and the Very Naked Girl: Movies from Cleo to

Clyde (Chicago: Holt, Rinehart and Winston, 1968).
T.V. Guide to the Movies (Toronto: Popular Library, 1974).

Reviews

Appeared in the New York *Herald Tribune* during the 1940s and 1950s; *New York* magazine from 1968–75; *The Washingtonian;* and *Palm Springs Life.* Crist began reviewing for *T.V. Guide* in 1965, and her work continues to appear there and in *Saturday Review,* until its demise in August 1982.

CROCE, ARLENE

Book

The Fred Astaire and Ginger Rogers Dance Book (New York: Random House, 1972).

Reviews and Articles

Have appeared in *Sight and Sound* and *Film Quarterly.*

DAWSON, JAN

A monograph, *Wim Wenders,* with Wim Wenders (New York: Zoetrope, 1977).

Reviews and Articles

Have appeared since the late-1960s in *Sight and Sound, Film Comment, Monthly Film Bulletin, Cinema Papers,* and *The New Statesman.*

DEREN, MAYA

Books

An Anagram of Ideas on Art, Form and Film (New York: The Alicat Bookshop Press, 1946). A theoretical text on Deren's notions of art and film making.
The Legend of Maya Deren, a three-volume documentary biography of Deren, edited by Clark, Hodson, Neiman, and Bailey, to be published by *Film Culture.*

Reviews and Articles

Replacing Jonas Mekas, Deren wrote a guest column for the *Village Voice* during the summer of 1961. *Film Culture* (no. 39) collects much of Deren's work (along with the writing of Ron Rice).

Articles

"Cinematography: The Creative Use of Reality," *Daedalus* (winter 1960). "Cinema as an Art Form," in Lewis Jacobs, ed. *Introduction to the Art of the Movies* (New York: Noonday Press, 1960).

Films

Meshes of the Afternoon (1943)
At Land (1944)
Ritual in Transfigured Time (1946)
Witches Cradle (1948)

The Very Eye of Night (1959)

DIDION, JOAN

Books

Slouching Towards Bethlehem (Farrar, Straus and Giroux, 1968). Essays on
 John Wayne, southern California, various directors.
The White Album (New York: Simon and Schuster, 1979). Essay on Hollywood.

Articles and Essays

Didion wrote a column, "The Coast," for *Esquire* in the mid-1970s. Other work
has appeared in *Vogue,* the *New York Times,* the *Saturday Evening Post,* and
the *New York Review of Books* (see especially "Letter from *Manhattan,*"
NYRB, August 17, 1979).

Screenplays (with John Gregory Dunne)

A Star is Born (1976)
True Confessions (1981)

H.D. [Hilda Doolittle]

Books

HERmione (New York: New Directions, 1981). Autobiographical novel.
Tribute to Freud (New York: McGraw-Hill, 1975).

Reviews

Appeared in *Close Up* during the years 1929–33.

Films

Wing Beat (1927) (preserved)
Foothills (1929) (preserved)
Monkey's Moon (1929) ("lost").

General

Pamphlet: "*Borderline:* A Pool Film with Paul Robeson" (London: 1930), an
 unsigned pamphlet, definitely attributable to H.D.

EISNER, LOTTE

Eisner worked with Henri Langlois to set up Cinématèque Française. As of this
writing, she was working on its administrative council.

Books

*The Haunted Screen: Expressionism in the German Cinema and the Influence of
 Max Reinhardt,* (Paris: 1952, André Bonne, 1952; Berkeley: University of Cal-
 ifornia Press, 1973, Roger Greaves, trans.).
Murnau (Paris: Le Terrain Vague, 1964; Berkeley: University of California
 Press, 1973).
Fritz Lang, Gertrude Mander, trans. and David Robinson, ed. (New York: Ox-
 ford University Press, 1977).

Reviews and Articles

Eisner was film reviewer and correspondent for a number of German and French newspapers and magazines during the 1930s and 1940s including Berlin's *Film-Kurier.* Her articles appeared in *Sight and Sound, Cahiers du Cinéma,* and *Films in Review* during the 1940s, 1950s and 1960s.

FERGUSON, OTIS

The Film Criticism of Otis Ferguson, Robert Wilson, ed. (Philadelphia: Temple University Press, 1971)

GILL, BRENDAN

Here at the New Yorker (New York: Random House, 1975). An insider's view of the workings of the magazine and its writers. Includes brief but complimentary portraits of Penelope Gilliatt and Pauline Kael.

GILLIATT, PENELOPE

Books

Three-Quarter Face: Reports and Reflections (New York: Coward, McCann and Geoghegan, 1980). A collection of reviews and portraits for the *New Yorker* (however, it does not include the notorious piece on Graham Greene).
Tati (London: Woburn Press, 1976).
Jean Renoir: Essays, Conversations, and Reviews (New York: McGraw-Hill, 1975).
Unholy Fools, Wits, Comics, Disturbers of the Peace: Film and Theater (New York: Viking, 1973). A collection of theater and film reviews.
Screenplay: *Sunday Bloody Sunday* (New York: Viking, 1971).
The Cutting Edge (New York: Coward, McCann and Geoghegan, 1979). A novel.
A State of Change (New York: Random House, 1967). A novel.
One by One (New York: Atheneum, 1966). A novel.

Reviews

Appeared in the London *Observer* (1961–67) and *The New Yorker* (1967–79).

GREENE, GRAHAM

The Pleasure Dome: The Collected Film Criticism, 1935–40 (Oxford and New York: Oxford University Press, 1980). The introduction details the difficulties—and rewards—of writing film reviews on deadline while working on other, more "major" projects.

HASKELL, MOLLY

Books

From Reverence to Rape: The Treatment of Women in the Movies (New York: Holt, Rinehart and Winston, 1973). Still a classic because of its original perception of women's cinematic roles as having deteriorated even more than their original chivalric concept. Haskell may be credited with the appearance of 'women's films" in the late-1970s.

Reviews and Articles

Have appeared in the *Village Voice, Film Comment, Film Heritage, Viva, Ms.,* and *New York.* Her work continues to appear in *Ms., Playgirl,* and *Vogue.*

HOUSTON, PENELOPE

Books

The Contemporary Cinema 1945–63 (New York and London: Penguin, 1963).

Reviews and Articles

Have appeared in *Sight and Sound* since 1949, where Houston has been an editor since 1951. Her column, "Scripting," ran in the magazine in 1951.

JACOBS, DIANE

Hollywood Renaissance (New York: A.S. Barnes, 1977). The first booklength treatment of Cassavetes, Altman, Coppola, Scorcese, and Mazursky.
But We Need the Eggs: The Magic of Woody Allen (New York: St. Martin's, 1982).

Reviews and Articles

Have appeared in *American Film, Film Comment,* and the *Soho News.*

JOHNSTON, CLAIRE

British structuralist-feminist.

Edited Works

Notes on Women's Cinema (London: Society for Education in Film and Television, 1973).
The Work of Dorothy Arzner: Towards a Feminist Cinema (London: British Film Institute, 1975).

Articles

With Pam Cook, "The Place of Women in the Films of Raoul Walsh," *Raoul Walsh,* Phil Hardy, ed. (Edinburgh Film Festival, 1974). Have also appeared in *Screen, Spare Rib.*

KAEL, PAULINE

Except for some early reviews for *City Lights,* the San Francisco magazine, almost all of Kael's work has been collected.

Books

I Lost It At the Movies (Boston: Little, Brown, 1965).
Kiss Kiss Bang Bang (Boston: Little, Brown, 1968).
Going Steady (Boston: Little, Brown, 1970).
Raising Kane: The Citizen Kane Book (Boston: Little, Brown, 1971). In which Kael makes many of her points with photographs, something she rarely does.

Deeper Into Movies (Boston: Little, Brown, 1973).
Reeling (Boston: Little, Brown, 1976).
When the Lights Go Down (New York: Holt, Rinehart and Winston, 1980).

Reviews and Articles

Kael reviewed for the *New Republic* (1967-68), *McCall's* (1966), and *The New Yorker* (1968-79, 1980—). Her articles and essays have appeared in *The Moviegoer, Film Culture, Filmkulcher,* the *Massachusetts Review, Sight and Sound,* and *Partisan Review.*

KAY, KARYN

Women and the Cinema: A Critical Anthology, and Gerald Peary, eds. (New York: E.P. Dutton, 1977). An anthology of 45 articles by major writers; many are reprints or excerpts. No unifying theory is advanced.

KINDER, MARSHA

One of the more readable academic film critics writing on the subject of women and film.

Books

Close Up: A Critical Perspective on Film, with Beverle Houston (New York: Harcourt, Brace, Jovanovich, 1972). Provides a general introduction to film.
Self and Cinema: A Transformalist Perspective, with Beverle Houston (New York: Human Sciences Press, 1981).

Reviews and Articles

Have appeared in *Sight and Sound, Film Quarterly,* and *Film Comment.* See especially "Scenes From a Marriage," *Film Quarterly* 27, no. 2 (winter 1974-75) and "Reflections on *Jeanne Dielman,*" *Film Quarterly* 30, no. 4.

LEJEUNE, C.A. [Caroline]

The first woman film critic to be regularly published.

Books

Cinema (London: Robert Maclehose & Co., 1931). A fine survey of the state of the cinema from historical and contemporary perspectives.
For Filmgoers Only (London: Faber and Faber, 1934). A primer on what viewers should look for in films.
Chestnuts in Her Lap (London: Phoenix House, 1947). A collection of *Observer* reviews.
Thank You for Having Me (London: Hutchinson & Co., 1964). Lejeune's autobiography.

Reviews and Articles

Appeared in the *Manchester Guardian* (1922-28), the *Observer* (1928-73), and *Sight and Sound.*

LOUNSBURY, M.O.

The Origins of American Film Criticism: 1909–1939 (New York: Arno, 1973).
Reprint of the 1966 edition. Contains a brief treatment of Evelyn Gerstein.

MAGNY, CLAUDE-EDMONDE

The Age of the American Novel: The Film Aesthetics of Fiction Between the Two Wars (New York: Ungar, 1972).

MAILER, NORMAN

Marilyn: A Biography (New York: Grosset and Dunlap, 1973). For comparative purposes only.

MASLIN, JANET

Reviews and Articles

Has reviewed for the *New York Times* since 1977. Her reviews and articles have also appeared in the *Boston Phoenix, New Times,* and *Newsweek,* during the years 1971–77.

MELLEN, JOAN

Books

Women and Their Sexuality in the New Film (New York: Horizon, 1973).
Marilyn Monroe (New York: Galahad Books, 1973).
Filmguide to the Battle of Algiers (Bloomington: Indiana University Press, 1973).
Voices From the Japanese Cinema (New York: Liveright, 1975).
The Waves at Genji's Door: Japan Through its Cinema (New York: Pantheon, 1976).
The World of Luis Buñuel (New York: Oxford University Press, 1978).
Big Bad Wolves: Masculinity in American Film (New York: Pantheon, 1978).

Reviews and Articles

Have appeared in *Film Comment, Film Heritage, Cinéaste, Literature/Film Quarterly, Ms.,* and the *New York Times.*

MICHELSON, ANNETTE

Michelson was advisory editor for Praeger film and art books.

Reviews and Articles

Appeared in *Artforum,* mainly in the late-1960s, and in *October* since 1978; Michelson was guest editor for both publications, and art reviewer and editor for the *International Herald Tribune.*

MOORE, MARIANNE

Wrote film reviews for *Close Up* during the years 1927–33.

MULVEY, LAURA

Mulvey is a film maker (*Penthiselea*, 1974; *Amy!*, 1981; and *Riddles of the Sphinx*, 1977) and was coeditor, with Jon Halliday, of *Douglas Sirk* (Lancashire, England, 1972). Her articles include "Visual Pleasure and Narrative Cinema," *Screen* 16, no. 3 (autumn 1975), a frequently anthologized, watershed piece of feminist criticism. Her essays have appeared in *Spare Rib* and *Seven Days*.

NIN, ANAÏS

In Favor of the Sensitive Man and Other Essays (New York: Harcourt, Brace, Jovanovich, 1976). Contains film essays and occasional comments on film.

POWDERMAKER, HORTENSE

Hollywood: The Dream Factory; An Anthropologist Looks at the Movie-Makers (New York: Arno, 1979). Reprint of the 1950 edition published in Boston.

POWELL, DILYS

Film critic for the Sunday *London Times* since 1939, Powell's articles have also appeared in *Sight and Sound*.

RICHARDSON, DOROTHY

Wrote a column, "Continuous Performance," in *Close Up*, 1927–33.

ROSEN, MARJORIE

Book

Popcorn Venus: Women, Movies and the American Dream (New York: Coward, McCann and Geoghegan. 1973). More sociological, less intellectual than Molly Haskell's *From Reverence to Rape*.

Reviews and Articles

Have appeared in *Ms., Jump Cut, American Film*, and *Ladies Home Journal*.

ROSS, LILLIAN

Reporting (New York: Dodd, Mead, 1981). "Picture" is the longest essay in this collection of Ross's *New Yorker* pieces, and it's a step-by-step, revealing report of the making of John Huston's *The Red Badge of Courage*. Ross is especially sharp on Huston.

SAYRE, NORA

Film reviewer for the *New York Times* from 1972–73 and *The Nation* since 1975.

Books

Sixties Going On Seventies (New York: Arbor House, 1973). Contains cultural essays and political reportage.

Running Time: Films of the Cold War (New York: Dial, 1982). Chronicles America in the 1950s.

SONTAG, SUSAN

Books

Against Interpretation (New York: Farrar, Straus and Giroux, 1966). Essays on Bresson, Godard, and Resnais.
Styles of Radical Will (New York: Farrar, Straus and Giroux, 1969). Essays on Bergman, Godard, and theater-film comparisons.
On Photography (New York: Farrar, Straus and Giroux, 1977).
Under the Sign of Saturn (New York: Farrar, Straus and Giroux, 1980). Collection of essays.

Essays

Have appeared in *Film Quarterly, The Nation, Partisan Review, The New Yorker,* and the *New York Review of Books,* notably on directors Riefenstahl and Syberberg.

Films

Duet for Cannibals (1969)
Brother Carl (1972)
Promised Lands (1974)

SARRIS, ANDREW

Book

The American Cinema: Directors and Directions 1929–68 (New York: E.P. Dutton, 1969).

Articles

"Notes on the *Auteur* Theory in 1962," in *Film Culture Reader,* P. Adams Sitney, ed. (New York: Praeger, 1970).
"Notes on the *Auteur* Theory in 1970," *Film Comment* 6, no. 3 (fall 1970).
Commentary on directors appears frequently in the *Village Voice.*

STARR, CECILE

Discovering the Movies (New York: Van Nostrand and Reinhold, 1972).

STEENE, BIRGITTA

Ingmar Bergman (Seattle: University of Washington Press, 1968).

TRILLING, DIANA

Books

Claremont Essays (New York: Harcourt, Brace and World, 1964). See "The Death of Marilyn Monroe."

Mrs. Harris: The Death of the Scarsdale Diet Doctor (New York: Harcourt, Brace, Jovanovich, 1981). The troubles of Jean Harris, with some awesome social observations.

Essays

Have appeared in the *New York Times, Partisan Review,* and *The Nation.*

TYLER, PARKER

Books

Sex, Psyche, Etcetera in the Film (New York: Horizon, 1969).

The Hollywood Hallucination (New York: Simon and Schuster, 1970) Psycho-cultural. Quite good on "The Somnambules," from Theda Bara through Garbo and Joan Crawford.

Magic and Myth of the Movies (New York: Simon and Schuster, 1970).

WALKER, ALEXANDER

The Celluloid Sacrifice (New York: Hawthorn, 1966). Suggests that women stars are sacrificial victims of movies and the industry. With the exception of the feminist critics, not—oddly—an approach emphasized by many women film critics.

WILLIAMS, LINDA

Figures of Desire: A Theory and Analysis of Surrealist Film (Urbana, Ill.: University of Illinois Press, 1981).

WOMEN AND FILM

Journal published in Los Angeles and Berkeley from 1972-75. Devoted to topics dealing with women and film; critical of mainstream Hollywood films and the auteur theory.

Index

About the Author

Marsha McCreadie has published a number of articles on women and film topics in *Cinéaste, American Film, Literature/Film Quarterly,* the *Journal of Popular Film and Televison,* and *Notable American Women.* She reviews films for *Films in Review* and *Ms.* and wrote for "Books & Arts" of *The Chronicle of Higher Education.* She is the author of *The American Movie Goddess.* A graduate of Syracuse University, she holds a doctorate in literature from the University of Illinois in Urbana. She has taught at Rutgers University in Newark and at Iona College in New Rochelle where she is presently teaching courses on women in film. She lives in New York City.